The New Normal

A Diagnosis the Church Can Live With

The New Normal

A Diagnosis the Church Can Live With

Thomas E. Ingram

linenpublishing.com

Earth and points beyond.

The New Normal: A Diagnosis the Church Can Live With

Copyright © 2014 Thomas E. Ingram

ISBN 978-0-9908486-0-8

Version 1.1

All rights reserved. Except for brief excerpts for review purposes, no portion of this book may be reproduced or used in any form without written permission from the publisher.

Published by Linen Publishing

www.linenpublishing.com

For John, Virginia, Dean & Helen.

Don't just tell a good story.

Live a good story.

Let your life corroborate & not negate your words.

This is living that compels, resonates, & fascinates.

You need to be about this kind of living.

I need to be about this kind of living.

We need to be about this kind of living.[1]

Eugene Cho

---

[1] Eugene Cho - Facebook post

Table of Contents

Acknowledgements	**2**
Foreword	**4**
Prologue	**8**
Introduction	**12**
Part 1 - Patient History	**26**
Chapter 1 - Onset of the Condition	28
Chapter 2 - Adaptive Strategies	42
Part 2 – Diagnostic Testing	**68**
Chapter 3 – Test Results	70
Part 3 - Literature Review	**92**
Chapter 4 – Creation Semiotics	94
Chapter 5 – Understanding the Kingdom	110
Chapter 6 - The Identity of Jesus	122
Part 4 - Treatment Plan	**141**
Chapter 7 – Rehabilitation	143
Part 5 - Big Buts	**179**
Chapter 8 - Is Your Big But the Problem?	181
Part 6 - Conclusion	**221**
Chapter 9 - Conclusion	223
Afterword	**233**
Bibliography	**235**
Bible Sources	**239**

Acknowledgements

First of all, the highest of thanks must go to my wife Nancy for her tireless and enduring support of my work. Her encouragement and support are invaluable and without them you would not be reading this book today.

Thank you to Emily Ingram, and Alissa & Sean Monroe. It is one of the great joys of my life to be a part of your lives, and my hope for your futures can be found on each and every page of this book.

Thank you Leonard Sweet for your friendship, support, encouragement, and belief that things such as this book could possibly come out of me.

Thank you to my doctoral faculty advisor Roger Nam for encouraging me to stick with writing in the voice that comes naturally rather than attempting to write in ways that are not true to who I am.

Thank you Chuck Conniry and Loren Kerns of George Fox Evangelical Seminary for welcoming and encouraging me on my journey to a DMin.

Thank you Joyce Shelleman for daring to suggest to a student quite unsure of his abilities that he should consider working toward a doctorate, and also Nancy Kristiansen for fanning the flames of this enthusiastic learner.

Thanks to Dave Jewitt who after a seemingly random encounter at jury duty went on to become a trusted friend whose counsel helped clarify the journey to where I now stand.

Thank you Phil Smith for your encouragement, support and stimulating conversation.

Thank you to my enduring group of YODA's (Lee Bartel, Mike Cunningham, Steve Ellis, and Danny Kittinger) for walking together and encouraging one another to pursue God's plan for our lives.

Thank you to my friends Pat & Denise Bolding and Bill & Katy Hoppa for great food and conversation.

Thanks to my friends Mark Riddle and Ross Taylor for stimulating conversation and for sharing your lives with me.

Thanks to all those I am connected with via twitter and Facebook and the connections we maintain.

And, a special thanks to those who take the time to participate in the Ten Things Project who made this book possible.

And last, but certainly not least, thank you to my crowd of advisors Robin Brush, Bryce Ashlin-Mayo, Dottie Escobedo-Frank, Bill Gibson, Dave Groenenboom, Vern Hyndman, Todd Littleton, Mark McNees, David Parker, and Billy Watson who very graciously agreed to read this manuscript prior to publication, offering the gift of their experience and insight as a way to help make this a better book. Your commitment to Jesus in living out your faith is an inspiration.

And thank you for taking the time to read this book and help uncover ways in which we might more faithfully manifest the Body of Christ on this earth.

Thomas Ingram

Foreword

In 1901, the United States was classified as the healthiest nation in the world among one hundred nations studied. By 1920, the United States had dropped to second place; by 1950 to third place. By 1970, forty-first place. And by 1981, of the one hundred healthiest nations in the world, the United States had dropped all the way to ninety-fifth place. (By 2013, we'd clawed our way back up to thirty-third place----or perhaps sixty-two other countries simply stopped trying). How do we go from being #1 to #95?

Recently, I was asked to rate a job candidate by choosing one of four responses to each question. The first optional response was "I Don't Know," which I always appreciate, because there are lots of things I don't know about (especially about people I'm asked to recommend). The next response was "Unacceptable." Next up the ladder was "Needs Improvement." And then came the top rung of the ladder, the highest level of approbation available to a reviewer: "Acceptable."

This is where we've come: our highest aspiration is not the "more excellent way" (1 Corinthians 12:31 NASB) but the "acceptable way." We may disagree about what constitutes a "more excellent way," and part of the fun of life--part of taste making, or curating our second nature, or forming our character----is debating this very question. But whatever we ultimately decide qualifies as excellence; "acceptable" is not acceptable. Jesus wants to release your best, not your mediocrity, on the world.

In his look at the "new normal" for the church, Thomas Ingram diagnoses the condition of a church that manages to Laodicea everything — instead of being hot (pursuing excellence) or being cold (failing spectacularly), we settle for being tepid. Churches who live with a tepid, fetid faith are never "on fire" about anything. They merely smolder and throw off smoke that chokes and clears the throat of all those who come close to them. God warns all tepid churches, and followers, that "because you are medium/mediocre/tepid/lukewarm/average, I will vomit you out of my mouth" (Revelation 3:16, paraphrased). In other words, be hot or get hurled.

Ingram not only diagnoses the symptoms and causes of the church's ailing condition, but he proposes a whole "new normal" based on the "more excellent way" of Jesus' "new kingdom life." Jesus insisted on a sense of the outside (as in "outside the norm") as well as a sensitivity to the outsider. It is time to lift up our heads, put our eyes on the mountains, and reach for the skies: "I will lift up mine eyes unto the hills, from whence does my help come? My help comes from the Lord who made heaven and earth" (Psalm 121). Enchantment comes when you close the door on the realities of the pantry and host a vision of the future based on hope and dreams.

One medieval commentator argued that the Hebrew prohibition against plowing a field with an ox and ass yoked together (Deuteronomy 22:10) is not because of the cruelty to the ass, but the cruelty to the ox whose greatness is being hindered. The ox is the king of domesticated animals, and is capable of immense feats and force. For it to be yoked with a beast only capable of much less is cruel and unjust. The "new normal" of the ox must not be hampered or hamstrung by the "new normal" of the ass. In reminding us of the "new kingdom life" offered by Jesus the Christ, Ingram forces us to dream some God-sized dreams for the church and for discipleship.

It appears I have "yummy" tastes. Japanese scientists have identified a fifth taste to set alongside salty, sweet, sour, and bitter. Halfway between soy and chestnut, it is actually called "yummy." When I indulge my taste for cheesecake, dulce de leche is my downfall. But it's more than caramel, milk, and sugar cooked to a burnt color. Dulce de leche is a "yummy" way of being a disciple-—an attitude toward church, community, and the world that says, "Jesus doesn't call you to lead an ordinary life."

Thomas Ingram has written a "yummy" book that calls the church and every disciple to go beyond the "ordinary" to live the "extraordinary" where Christ's kingdom is lived now "on earth, as it is in heaven."

Leonard Sweet

Prologue

The journey that has resulted in this book initially began with a problem I was having entering into conversations about faith issues with my non-Christian friends, for whenever we would get close to the topic of Christianity, they would start to tense up and sometimes even get angry. They weren't angry with me…we were friends, but they were still angry. I made the assumption this phenomenon was not unique to my situation, which got me thinking. Had the culture wars gotten so intense that even a casual discussion about Christianity with non-Christian friends was no longer possible due to the cultural mine fields now surrounding the topic?

And so, in an effort to answer this question, I decided to do what any rational Christian would do (read ironic sarcasm here): I created an online forum where non-Christians could vent their frustrations concerning Christians or the Church. This project included 3 web sites. There was the master site – tenthingsproject.com and the two secondary sites – tenthingsihateaboutchurch.com and tenthingsihateaboutchristians.com. The sites are still operational, although I am not paying Google Ads to push people in their direction any longer.

In designing the sites, a challenge arose in determining how to collect the data. If I created categories, I would be leading and directing the answers to some degree. For example, if I created categories for *worship style* or *message* or *friendliness* or whatever, I would be directing answers to those areas and possibly missing categories of greater importance. This would make the results easier to tabulate, but it could also limit or skew the results in pre-determined directions.

So, in an effort to complicate the research, while at the same time getting a better indication of their true objections, I chose to let each individual come up with their own *ten things* apart from pre-determined categories. This decision ultimately delayed my efforts to work through the data for quite some time, for I knew the randomness I had created was going to cost me in time and frustration. However, in the end I just decided to approach it the same way one would approach eating an elephant…one bite at a time.

The Research

During the first 6 months the tenthingsproject.com site logged 825 contributions from individuals all over the country from a wide variety of age groups including teenagers, retirees, and everything in between. But, there was a strange turn of events about to unfold I did not see coming. While I had created the sites to provide a space where non-Christians could vent their frustrations with the Church and Christians, surprisingly 86% of those contributing to the site self-identified as Christians with 8% of those turning out to be Church staff members. This caught me by surprise, but in the end was much more interesting than the direction I was originally heading with this project.

There were, of course, those who questioned the purpose of the tenthingsproject.com and the sanity of whoever created such an abomination on the web. And, there was one guy who was suspicious of the site, expecting it to lead to some sort of financial or evangelistic appeal at the end (where would he ever get that idea?). However, in spite of these isolated reservations, most of the contributors were more than happy to let fly on the organizations to which they belong and their Christian compatriots. As a result, a treasure trove of information emerged from my crowd of volunteers. The book you are about to read has been written in an effort to not only honor the collective voice of those who contributed to the websites but also to help identify some of the ways we might overcome the challenges they so enthusiastically made crystal clear.

A couple items of note: since the Church is comprised of Christians, for our discussion here, we will treat the two as one entity. So when we are discussing the Church, we are discussing the Christians that make up the Church as well, and vice versa.

This book is written and presented in a way that will hopefully be informative to both ministry professionals and non-professionals. Advice was given that I should choose to write to one group or the other. Taking advice has never been one of my strong points. So, for the ministry professional or perhaps academic, I hope the streams of thought are deep enough to encourage you to dive deeper into the issues. And, for the non-professional, I hope the material is presented in such a way that inspires you to engage in a little "kingdom" living.

Introduction

My wife Nancy is a Diagnostic Neurophysiologist. I love telling people this because it typically elicits a rather blank stare, which gives me space to tell them about the amazing things she does on a daily basis. I know they are amazing because I get to hear the stories over dinner each evening. Patient confidentiality is of course paramount, but the story of someone's life and situation need not include names or addresses to be compelling.

Nancy's patients are primarily those who find themselves in a place where their capabilities and capacities are on the decline due to some sort of neurological dysfunction resulting from trauma, disease, poor choices, or perhaps aging. These patients arrive at her office in a variety of emotional states ranging from scared, confused, and desperate to angry, resentful, and demanding. But in spite of their unique and individual situations, each of her patients have one thing in common: the severity of their condition has placed them in a position from which they can no longer deny the existence of their problem and must now seek help.

Nancy begins her diagnostic investigation by asking the patient questions...lots of questions... questions such as the following:

- What brings you here today?
- When did you first notice the problem?
- Did the symptoms come on you suddenly or gradually?
- Do you have any other related symptoms?

- What is the most debilitating aspect of your condition?
- How have these symptoms affected your life?
- What do you do to cope with the symptoms?
- Etc. Etc. Etc.

(When I asked her for a list of sample questions she gave me a list of 119 just for starters).

Her questions are very specific and intentional, for each one provides valuable pieces of information that contribute to a clear understanding of the problem. Interestingly, while each patient is unique in the way in which their condition manifests, oftentimes they progress through a fairly predictable sequence of events: *the onset of the condition, the pursuit of adaptive behaviors,* and *a precipitating event* that creates a sense of urgency causing them to *seek help.*

Many of the details concerning their dysfunction are revealed if one asks the right questions and then listens to what the patient says. Believe it or not, listening to the patient is a practice many do not have the inclination or the desire in which to engage. Fortunately for Nancy's patients, she is an active listener. As she listens she begins to understand her patient's condition, for the truth of their dysfunction is revealed in their stories. Once these stories are told and the history of dysfunction is understood, the diagnostic process moves forward toward *testing, reviewing the literature, diagnosis* and then *treatment.*

This brief explanation is of course an oversimplification of a complicated process learned over a period of many years in the clinical setting. However it does provide a framework from which we can better understand the diagnostic process, and subsequently the pathway to rehabilitation.

The treatment and rehabilitative strategies that enable recovery require work and sacrifice on the part of the patient. Oftentimes on this journey, the biggest decision facing the patient is whether they are going to accept their condition and diminishing prospects for the future as the **new normal** or envision and embrace an alternative **new normal; a new normal** in which they work to regain functionality they thought was lost forever.

Like many of my wife's patients, the Church has been suffering from a variety of conditions for many years. We see evidence of this not only in declining membership and attendance, but also in how Christian cultural influence has diminished to the point we are sliding dangerously close to cultural irrelevance. Some consider these symptoms to be the natural ebb and flow of the tides of culture or even the inevitable decline of an organization whose time has passed, but as the intensity of these symptoms increase under the pressure of postmodern sensibilities, even the most staunch defenders of the status quo are able to read the writing on the wall: Houston, we have a problem.

Some have chosen to deny the existence of a problem while others have engaged in adaptive strategies (more on this later) in an attempt to render our dysfunction unnoticeable to those around us while simultaneously claiming the Church was changing with the times.

These adaptive strategies, however, work against us in a variety of ways. First of all, adaptive strategies delay healing and rehabilitation, which results in a worsening of our condition. And secondly, adaptive strategies come with a cost.

In economics, there is a principle known as "opportunity cost." An opportunity cost is the value of an activity we cannot engage in because we are doing something else. For example; when I choose to go to work, I cannot go to the gym or any other activity I might choose to do instead of going to work. So, in going to work I lose the opportunity to go to the gym. As such, the opportunity cost of going to work is the lost opportunity (or value) of going to the gym.

In life we weigh various opportunity costs against one another all the time. As children we weigh the cost of doing something we are not supposed to do against the potential consequence losing dessert for a week. As teens we weigh the cost of not studying for an exam against the possibility of getting a better grade if we were to stay home from the party and do the work. And, as adults we weigh the various options in almost every area of our lives as more and more choices concerning what to do with our time creep into the landscape of our lives.

Opportunity cost relates to our current discussion in that the time and energy the church invests maintaining adaptive strategies in an attempt to accommodate our dysfunction rather than working toward improving our situation, are time and energy that could have been used more effectively and honestly to engage our culture in the work of Christ. Unfortunately, these lost opportunities also come with a secondary consequence in that they further contribute to our slide toward cultural irrelevancy.

As our adaptive strategies are failing the church, more and more of us are finding ourselves at a crossroads…a landscape from which we must confront the reality of our situation. As with my wife's patients, it is time to make the difficult decisions. Do we accept our condition as the *new normal*; the natural trajectory of an institution whose best days are behind it. Or, or do we do the hard work required of us to restore our collective health and halt this descent into cultural irrelevancy? In either case, the decision made will determine our *new normal*.

Clinical Examples

Before we proceed with our diagnostic investigation into the current state of the Church, let's first consider how the road to dysfunction plays out in a few afflictions we are perhaps more familiar with such as hearing loss, obesity, dizziness, failing memory, and pain.

Hearing Loss

There is an old story that goes something like this: A husband was concerned his wife might be losing her hearing, so he made an appointment to talk over the situation with their family doctor. At the appointment, the man asked the doctor if there was any way he could confirm the existence of his wife's hearing problem apart from bringing her in for an appointment. In response, the doctor told him to perform the following experiment when he got home. "When your wife is not looking in your direction, stand about 15 feet away and ask her a question in a normal voice. If she does not answer, move up five feet and ask again. Continue this process until she answers. This will give you some idea concerning the degree of her hearing loss." When the man got home, his wife was preparing dinner in the kitchen. He thought this would be a perfect time to perform his test. So, he stood at the doorway to the kitchen and asked his wife what was for dinner…no answer. He moved up 5 feet and asked again…still no answer. He moved up another 5 feet until he was standing directly behind her and asked one more time. This time his wife turned around and rather indignantly said: "For goodness sakes. I have told you 2 times already: meatloaf and mashed potatoes."

This story underscores one of the initial obstacles we face when experiencing a gradual decline in functionality: we think the problem is someone else's problem, and we continue to think it is someone else's problem until it becomes painfully obvious the problem is indeed our own. It would be logical to assume once we have been made aware of a problem such as hearing loss, we would make efforts to seek help in overcoming it. Unfortunately, more often than not, this is not the first strategy of choice.

In the example of our unsuspecting husband in the story above, rather than make an appointment to visit the hearing aid specialist, he will more than likely push the responsibility for the problem off on those around him; asking everyone to repeat what was said until he can understand. While this can be effective to the degree people are willing to play along, ultimately this strategy not only delays pursuit of a better solution, but also allows his condition to continue to deteriorate.

There is also a technological variant to our hearing story that can become obvious when perhaps visiting the home of a grandparent or aging neighbor as we notice it getting harder and harder to carry on a conversation above the ever increasing volume of the television. This is a less risky strategy and perhaps more attractive to the person with hearing loss in that it does not require the participation of others…only themselves and the television remote…a strategy which ultimately enables them to remain in control. However, like all adaptive strategies, it comes with a cost: it prolongs the condition and contributes to the worsening of the situation (and his relationships).

Adaptive strategies such as these also carry an additional consequence: as the individual's condition worsens, they typically begin to withdraw from social interaction in an attempt to minimize the confrontation and embarrassment that increasingly accompanies their inability to hear. This strategy will likely continue until there is some sort of precipitating event that increases the attractiveness of pursuing a better option. Oftentimes the alternate solution arrives in the form of a demand from those who care most about this individual; a demand that the person with diminishing hearing accept the reality of their situation and do something about it. It is at this point the person with hearing loss runs out of options and is most likely to seek help.

Obesity

Obesity is another challenge facing many of us in the West as our prosperity and abundance affects us in counterproductive ways. There are instances in which rapid weight gain can be an early indicator or some sort of malady, but in most cases, it grows on us gradually.

Those of us who find ourselves in this position may initially attempt to deny or ignore our increase in geography or perhaps try to explain the weight away by suggesting it's just a temporary thing; we have not been eating right due to some stress in the family or at work; but as soon as we get through this, things will begin to settle down and we will eat better. Or, maybe we even go on the offensive, telling people to just quit talking to us about it, suggesting that if they weren't constantly nagging us about our weight, maybe we wouldn't eat as much. Again, these are attempts to shift responsibility for the problem onto some external circumstance or individual.

As the weight begins to accumulate, we may move on to a different kind of adaptive strategy, moving from health to stealth as it were; dressing differently in hopes of obscuring the obvious. This strategy can be successful in delaying the moment of truth, but ultimately as the weight continues to pile on, we will likely withdraw from those around us and their judgmental eyes so we can spend more quality time with our favorite ice cream. Unfortunately, the precipitating event that typically causes us to take action in this scenario is some sort of health crisis, or perhaps the announcement from someone near and dear to us that they will leave us if we don't do something about our condition. At this point we have to either accept our situation and subsequent isolation from those we know and love as the *new normal*, or take steps toward a *new normal* that doesn't weigh quite so heavily upon us.

Dizziness

Dizziness is a symptom associated with a variety of conditions brought about by an equal variety of causes. While it can come on us suddenly, resulting from some sort of physical trauma or medical emergency, more often than not, dizziness comes upon us gradually...beginning as a slightly annoying inconvenience and progressing to a condition that prevents even the strongest of us from being able to move about our world. Initially, we may try to ignore the symptoms and deflect attention away from its increasing presence by suggesting our momentary loss of the horizon occurred because we just stood up too fast, or perhaps resulted from our misstep or a need to get new shoes with better footing or support. As our condition worsens, we learn a variety of adaptive behaviors such as touching a wall when walking for added stability or modifying our gait to smaller steps in an effort to keep us on our feet. Ironically, both of these adaptations tend to exacerbate the situation and hasten our decline.

As our condition continues to worsen and our ability to maneuver correspondingly declines, we predictably begin to withdraw from social interaction, retreating to the safety of our private cocoon. Unfortunately, it is typically a fall that not so gently prompts us to abandon this strategy and confront the reality of our situation. At this point however, the damage has been done and the *new normal* we are faced with is one that could likely have been mitigated if we had only sought help sooner.

Failing Memory

Many of us have experienced this condition at close range in the lives of our parents or grandparents as their aging begins to take its toll on their capabilities and their identity gradually slips from their grasp. We often hear this talked about as a type of Alzheimer's but in reality there are a variety of dementias that can rob us of the understanding of who we are and subsequently, the ability to successfully interact in this world.

This malady follows a similar trajectory to the other conditions we have discussed in that the individual tends to ignore the condition as long as they can, possibly making excuses such as: "who can remember everything," or "I just have too much on my mind." At first they might even joke about their forgetfulness, attempting to laugh it off up to the point they realize it is not a laughing matter.

As their cognitive ability continues to decline, they can attempt to mitigate its impact by living in a world of sticky notes; each one a reminder of something that must be done and should not be forgotten. Or perhaps, they just try to maintain as best they can until the imagined day when they wake up from this nightmare and can return to the way things were. Unfortunately, as their grasp of reality continues to slip away, they typically become fearful and react in ways we have seen in the previous examples: withdrawing from social interaction and isolating themselves from what appears like an increasing opportunity to fail. It is rare that the person experiencing this decline is the one to suggest seeking help, for help typically comes in the form of a concerned son or daughter and results in the removal of the individual from their home and relocation in a safe place where they can live out the remainder of their days.

Pain

Pain, like some of the other maladies we have discussed, is typically a symptom of a condition rather than a condition in and of itself. In spite of this, we oftentimes treat pain as a condition, assuming if we can ignore it or medicate it away, the underlying cause of the pain is not something that should concern us.

A sudden onset of pain is something that can get our attention though, and this event typically elicits a rather speedy trip in the direction of the nearest emergency room (think appendicitis here). In contrast, a gradually increasing pain creeps to the forefront of our consciousness over a period of days, weeks, months, or years, as it somehow remains below the radar, becoming just another one of the things we learn to deal with.

In the early stages, we may try to ignore it, hoping it is just a temporary thing, saying that it doesn't hurt that bad in hopes that tomorrow will be a better day. Or, we may try to self-medicate it away for a period of time in one of the many ways available to us...both legal and not so legal. But once again, as the pain level increases we tend to withdraw from activities that might increase or bring the pain upon us. Eventually we reach the point where either our attempts to self-medicate or perhaps the pain medication ceases to do its job, forcing us to acknowledge the severity of our situation and seek help. Pain has a way of eventually motivating us to take action.

Parallels to the Body of Christ

We took a moment to consider these physical maladies so that we might better understand the current condition of our Church, for in a metaphorical sense, this collective "we" that manifests as this Body of Christ is suffering from a variety of symptoms similar to those discussed above:

• Just as the progression of hearing loss in our patient results in a gradual withdrawal from engagement with others, churches oftentimes turns a deaf ear in the direction of an accusatory culture as we retreat to the safety of our sanctuaries…an echo chamber in which our own voices have priority and where we are able to ignore the cultural taunts that tend to undermine our fragile self-image.

• Just like the obese patient who seeks to obscure the enormity of their problem in a variety of ways, many churches pursue a similar strategy when we attempt to obscure our dissatisfaction by offering a seemingly endless buffet of opportunities in hopes of presenting a picture of ourselves as a healthy and vibrant church.

• Just like the dizzy patient who upon finding their world spinning out of control, reduces their level of engagement in hopes of minimizing their symptoms, we as the Church are finding ourselves reeling on unstable and unfamiliar cultural terrain, unable to adjust our footing fast enough to successfully negotiate the challenges we face on the ever-changing cultural landscape.

• Just like the patient whose memory deteriorates until they are ultimately unable to remember who they are or how to function in this world, we too are forgetting who we are in

Christ and losing our ability to successfully interact with the culture in which we live.

• And finally, just like the patient who attempts to ignore, tolerate, or self-medicate their pain away, we as the Church have ignored, tolerated, or seemingly medicated the growing awareness of our condition away as long as possible and now find ourselves at a crossroads.

To those who willingly embrace the status quo, I hope the information presented and stories told will challenge you to re-evaluate your present position.

But, to those of you who are anxious to become the voice of the loved one, willing to intercede on behalf of the patient (the Church), this book will hopefully clarify the depth of our dysfunction while at the same time provide you with a variety of interventional strategies to help breathe life back into our ailing Church.

To accomplish this we will take an approach similar to the one utilized by my wife in her medical practice as we attempt to diagnose an ailing Body of Christ.

• We will take a good look at the history of the patient (the Church), as we uncover the contributing factors to our tenuous position.

• We will examine our test results and review the literature on the subject (in this case Scripture) so that we might better understand not only our current condition but also understand what a healthy Body looks like.

• Rather that accept the present condition of the church as the *new normal*, we will propose a treatment plan that points to a different *new normal*… one in which the church is a thriving and vibrant light shining on the hill, illuminating and infiltrating the cultural landscape with the love of Christ.

• We will then discuss the challenges that confront us on the road to rehabilitation, drawing upon the stories of those who have gone before us to inspire us to pursue a *new normal*…a new normal the Church can live with.

Part 1 - Patient History

Chapter 1 - Onset of the Condition

Diagnostic Strategy: What Brings You Here Today?

Many a book has been written about the current state of dysfunction in the Church and each of them provides an in-depth discussion of their particular perspective on the issue. Rather than review the current literature on the subject in an effort to build the case that many have built before, let's just assume anyone with a pulse is at least somewhat aware of the fact that the position the church currently maintains in the culture is somewhat diminished from the space it once occupied. We see evidence of this in a variety of ways:

• The separation between church and state is currently more accurately described as a chasm... a geography from which neither side appears either willing or able to successfully engage the other.

• Denominational divides are increasingly precarious, as we seem more and more inclined to fortify the geography on which we take our theological stands rather than work together on those things we hold in common.

• Church attendance is on the decline as increasing numbers people identify themselves with the non-believing side of the current spiritual buffet rather than associate themselves with an institution that seems unable to sufficiently defend itself against the onslaught of postmodernity.

• Those who would consider themselves regular attenders of church are found woefully absent from any activities other than a somewhat sporadic appearance at the occasional Sunday morning worship service.

Houston, we have a problem.

Did the symptoms come on us suddenly or gradually?

Sudden onset of dysfunction within the church is not very common, but it does occur and when it does it is typically self-inflicted: brought about, for example, when a pastor is arrested in a rather compromising position or perhaps when a church assumes a stance of judgment rather than one of grace in the community. The sudden arrival of such a problem typically encourages a church to bypass the pursuit of adaptive strategies. Instead it takes immediate action in hopes of mitigating the negative consequences that result from such an event. In addition to these acts of self-preservation, the church hopefully finds within its collective heart the ability to rehabilitate and restore the unfortunate individual who stands at the center of the controversy. However, as we all know, more often than not we tend to release our wounded to pursue other opportunities in an attempt to distance our church from the appearance of impropriety. While this strategy seems to fly in the face of all we consider "holy," our first response when injured tissue is found in the Body is unfortunately to remove it as soon as possible, separating it from the life giving tissue that is meant to support and sustain it so healing can occur.

While these very public manifestations of dysfunction do occur, the majority of problems currently tormenting the Church have risen to prominence gradually over hundreds of years. A desire for expediency might encourage us to reduce the window of time we consider relevant to the development of our current condition, however unless we pause to consider how we got here, we fall victim to allowing the enormity of our current state of affairs to mask the ongoing influence the past maintains on the present.[2] And so, to better understand the history of our patient (the Church), let's now look at some of the events that have contributed to the development of our ecclesial dysfunction.

In the Beginning

When did you first notice your symptoms?

On a mountaintop in Galilee, post-resurrection Jesus revealed his plan for the disciples:

"All authority in heaven and on earth has been given to me. Go therefore and make disciples of all nations, baptizing them in the name of the Father and of the Son and of the Holy Spirit, and teaching them to obey everything that I have commanded you. And remember, I am with you always, to the end of the age."[3]

And, in Acts we find Jesus' final recorded admonition:

"You will receive power when the Holy Spirit has come upon you; and you will be my witnesses in Jerusalem, in all Judea and Samaria, and to the ends of the earth."[4]

Shortly after delivering this message, Jesus was lifted up into heaven. It's not hard to imagine the Apostles were curious about what Jesus meant and how this Holy Spirit would manifest, but after their years of walking alongside Jesus, if they

---

[2] Brad S. Gregory, *The Unintended Reformation: How a Religious Revolution Secularized Society* (Cambridge, Mass.: Belknap Press of Harvard University Press, 2012), 7.
[3] Matthew 28:18-20.
[4] Acts 1:8.

had learned anything, they had likely learned that in time, their murky understanding would eventually become clear; so they waited. They waited seven weeks from Passover to Pentecost...and then it happened:

> *"When the day of Pentecost had come, they were all together in one place. And suddenly from heaven there came a sound like the rush of a violent wind, and it filled the entire house where they were sitting. Divided tongues, as of fire, appeared among them, and a tongue rested on each of them. All of them were filled with the Holy Spirit and began to speak in other languages, as the Spirit gave them ability."*[5]

After this promised manifestation of the Holy Spirit, Peter (the same Peter that had weeks earlier denied even knowing Jesus) boldly delivered a brief sermon that resulted in 3000 new believers[6] as the Holy Spirit began to announce the presence of something new on this earth: the Church. Interestingly, as this new Church began to reproduce and expand, it was "not as much interested in 'kingdom building' as it was 'in kingdom living,'"[7] living in a place where the "the dynamic presence and power of the Holy Spirit was found in a community of the Spirit rather than in a sanctuary of stone and glass."[8] In other words, it was not necessary for the life of this new body of believers to be dependent upon a physical temple or sanctuary because (as they were learning) *"you are the temple of God, and God himself is present in you."*[9]

---

[5] Acts 2:1-4.
[6] Acts 2:41.
[7] Ray S. Anderson, *An Emergent Theology for Emerging Churches* (Downers Grove, Ill.: IVP Books, 2006), 96.
[8] Ibid., 101.
[9] 1 Cor 3:16 (MSG).

The Church at this point in the story was primarily a Jewish institution until one of its greatest persecutors (Paul) was transformed into its most tireless missionary.[10] After Paul's rather dramatic conversion experience and temporary bout with blindness on the road to Damascus, Paul took the Good News of the Gospel to the Gentiles, founding churches wherever his travels took him. The worship activities in these new churches typically consisted of the "singing of Psalms and hymns, mutual exhortation and teaching, prophecy, glossolalia (praying in tongues) and healings."[11] But above and beyond the variety of ways in which the Christian community worshiped, they were primarily known for the way in which they lived, so much so that they were commonly referred to as people of the *way*[12]... likely a reference to Jesus' description of himself as "the *way*, and the truth, and the life."[13]

This tradition of Jesus' followers being known as people of The Way continued for five centuries, as Christianity was primarily known as a way of life rather than a doctrinal system or a promise of salvation[14] for "the church was not yet an institution, a building, or a system of theology; believers were the church, the Jesus followers - a holy people enacting a Christian way of life that had transformed their beings."[15]

---

[10] David Bentley Hart, *The Story of Christianity: An Illustrated History of 2000 Years of the Christian Faith* (London: Quercus Books, 2008), 26.
[11] Ibid., 30.
[12] Acts 9:2, Acts 18:25, Acts 19:9, Acts 19:23, Acts 24:14. Acts 24:14, Acts 24:22 (italics added)
[13] John 14:6. (italics added)
[14] Diana Butler Bass, *A People's History of Christianity: The Other Side of the Story*, 1 Reprint ed. (Philadelphia, Pa.: HarperOne, 2010), 27.
[15] Bass, *A People's History of Christianity*, 75.

The Greek word for the word *way* in the New Testament means "way, road, journey, custom."[16] As such, we see Christianity being known as the *way* in which these followers of Jesus (these little Christs aka Christians) lived, the *road* on which they engaged this *journey* of life, and the *customs* associated with that way being "authenticated through a life of dedication."[17]

However, as is true with most groups that expand and grow, issues arise that must be settled if the group is going to have some sort of continuity and remain true to its ideals. The first example we have of this occurs in the book of Acts when a group of individuals from Judea arrived at Antioch teaching new believers *"unless you are circumcised according to the custom of Moses, you cannot be saved."*[18] Paul and Barnabas immediately protested, but were apparently thought without proper authority to decide the issue, so they left for Jerusalem in order to get a ruling from the Apostles.[19] After some debate, the Apostles determined and announced a minimal set of standards that must be adhered to by these new Gentile followers of the Way: *"abstain only from things polluted by idols and from fornication and from whatever has been strangled and from blood."*[20]

Upon Paul and Barnabas's return to Antioch from this meeting they were able to give these new believers the good news at which the Bible says they *"rejoiced at the exhortation."*[21]

---

[16] Robert Young, *Young's Analytical Concordance to the Bible* (Peabody: Hendrickson Publishers 01/01/, 2005), 103.
[17] David E. Fitch, *The Great Giveaway: Reclaiming the Mission of the Church from Big Business, Parachurch Organizations, Psychotherapy, Consumer Capitalism, and Other Modern Maladies* (Grand Rapids, MI: Baker Books, 2005), 32.
[18] Acts 15:1.
[19] Acts 15:2.
[20] Acts 15:19-20.
[21] Acts 15:31.

The Message says it a little differently: *"The people were greatly relieved and pleased."*[22] I bet they were…at least the men.

In this story, we have the first example of the new Church attempting to work out disagreements over proper doctrine in a thoughtful and consistent manner. However, this was not the end of disparate views over orthodoxy nor was the Church always able to settle its disagreements with such an amicable approach, as many of the disagreements in the history of the early Church unfortunately rose above the level of thoughtful discussion and resulted in accusations of heresy. Some of these alternative interpretations of theology include those of the Gnostics, Marcion, and Arius.

The Gnostics, while anything but unified, believed they possessed a special kind of mystical knowledge; something that was only for those with a true understanding and that salvation was possible only through this special knowledge.[23] They believed that "spirit is good and matter is evil"[24] and subsequently believed that "Christ did not actually become incarnate as Jesus but only appeared to be human"[25] for in their view, the good spirit of God could not be contaminated as a physical presence.

For Marcion, the "Old Testament had no validity for Christians whatsoever, and he considered the God described in it a tribal, bloodthirsty demigod who did not deserve Christian adoration or worship."[26] He felt the Father of Jesus was not the

---

[22] Acts 15:31. (MSG)
[23] Justo L. Gonzalez, *The Story of Christianity, Volume 1: The Early Church to the Dawn of the Reformation* (Story of Christianity) (New York: HarperOne, 1984), 59.
[24] Bass, *A People's History of Christianity*, 37.
[25] Roger E. Olson, *The Story of Christian Theology: Twenty Centuries of Tradition and Reform* (New York: IVP Academic, 1999), 29.

same God as the God of the Old Testament[27] and proposed God the Father's original intent was there be only a spiritual world, but this intent was undermined when the God of the Old Testament created a physical world and placed mankind in it by either mistake or evil intent.[28] This understanding led Marcion to disavow the Old Testament as the "word of an inferior God."[29] In an effort to distance Christianity from this inferior God, Marcion promoted a canon free of "any taint of Judaism."[30] Even though "some early Christians clearly considered Marcion the arch-heretic and main enemy of orthodox and catholic Christianity,"[31] Marcion's ideologies lingered on for centuries.

It would be easy to think of these and other theological disputes as the lofty mental meanderings of the more learned of the day, but in Alexandria in 318 AD riots broke out in the streets over a theological disagreement that began between the bishop and a man named Arius.[32] Their disagreement boiled down to conflicting opinions concerning the nature of Jesus and the Logos incarnate within him.[33] Arius could not acknowledge that Jesus was both fully human and fully God. As such, many feared Arius was "denying any genuine sense of Christ's divinity and rejecting the Trinity entirely."[34] The difficulty for Arius arose from the view that "if the Son of God is truly God, then God cannot be immutable as all believe him to be because

---

[26] Ibid., 132.
[27] Gonzalez, *The Story of Christianity, Volume 1*, 61.
[28] Ibid.
[29] Ibid.
[30] Ibid., 133.
[31] Ibid.
[32] Ibid., 141.
[33] Ibid., 145.
[34] Ibid., 147.

the son changed through entering into history and suffering in the flesh of Jesus Christ."[35] In an effort to settle this dispute that was threatening to split the church, Constantine (the emperor of Rome and self-appointed head of the Church) ordered "all Christian bishops from throughout the empire to come to a meeting to settle this doctrinal dispute and decide exactly what it is that Christians must believe to be considered authentically Christian."[36] This discussion resulted in what we know today as the Nicene Creed.

However, the Nicene Creed was not the first attempt to clarify what one must believe to be considered Christian, for an earlier creed surfaced somewhere around 150 AD we know as the Apostles Creed.[37] Most of us are familiar with variations of the following:

> I believe in God the Father Almighty,
>
> maker of heaven and earth;
>
> And in Jesus Christ his only Son our Lord:
>
> who was conceived by the Holy Spirit,
>
> born of the Virgin Mary,
>
> suffered under Pontius Pilate,
>
> was crucified, dead, and buried;
>
> he descended into hell:
>
> the third day he rose from the dead;

---

[35] Ibid., 148.
[36] Ibid., 140.
[37] Geoffrey W. Bromiley, *The International Standard Bible Encyclopedia: A-D* (Grand Rapids, MI: Eerdmans Pub Co, 1995), 808.

he ascended into heaven,

and sitteth at the right hand of God the Father Almighty;

from thence he shall come to judge the quick and the dead.

I believe in the Holy Spirit,

the holy catholic church,

the communion of saints,

the forgiveness of sins,

the resurrection of the body,

and the life everlasting. Amen.

The Nicene Creed later revised this language to counter the Arian challenge in an attempt to clarify that God the Father and Jesus are indeed of one substance, underscoring both the existence of the Trinity and the nature of Christ. It might be easy for one to think the debates were now settled and the Church could get on with the business of being the Church, but that was not to be the case.

As the Church continued to grow and disperse over a larger geography, each area tended to lean on a different collection of authoritative documents for inspiration.

> "Some assemblies used nothing but the Greek version of the Hebrew Bible; some believed in nothing but the Gospels and rejected the Jewish scriptures of a common past; still others revered writings that told stories of Jesus that challenged doctrines espoused by church leaders who issued directives from places safely far away: Rome, Milan, Jerusalem."[38]

For obvious reasons, this strategy proved challenging. In an attempt to create an authoritative set of documents, which they could look to as canon, a variety of preferred collections were considered. The list containing all 27 books we know today as The Bible was proposed by Athanasius, bishop of Alexandria, in 367.[39] Later, in meetings at Hippo and Carthage in 393 and 397 respectively, Athanasius's list was affirmed and determined to be "final and authoritative."[40]

The tradition of arguing over proper doctrine and orthodoxy continues today and has resulted in the fracturing of our Church into approximately 33,000 different Christian denominations.[41] These disagreements not only serve to divide the church but also provide fodder for those whose reticence to embrace Christianity is grounded upon the premise that "if you guys as Christians can't even agree on what you believe, then why should I believe what you are trying to tell me?"

This enduring preoccupation of arguing about doctrine and what constitutes proper belief has contributed to our current state of dysfunction, landing us on a theological terrain from which we can profess our Christianity without actually having to do the hard work of being Christian. In other words, our *way* now lies at some distance from *The Way*.

Interestingly, in many *ways* we have fallen victim to the same misunderstandings that plagued the Gnostics, Marcion, and Arius:

---

[38] Prof. Lori Anne Ferrell, *The Bible and the People* (New York: Yale University Press, 2008), 7.
[39] Olson, *The Story of Christian Theology*, 135.
[40] Ibid., 135.
[41] Richard Ostling, "Researcher Tabulates World's Believers," Adherents, http://www.adherents.com/misc/WCE.html .

- Like the Gnostics, we tend to place a higher value on knowledge or allegiance to a primary set of beliefs as the benchmarks in the life of a Christian above living a life that actually provides evidence of Christ:

- Like Marcion, we attempt to distance the past from the present and the spiritual from the earthy when we place a higher emphasis on maintaining proper spiritual beliefs as compared to dealing with and caring for some our more earthy brothers and sisters.

- Like Arius who could not come to terms with a Jesus who was both fully human and fully God, we enthusiastically lift up a Jesus who died for our sins while at the same ignoring the Jesus who dared to walk amongst the muck and mire of humanity in an attempt to save them.

To follow Christ is not just to learn about him or "to learn from him, but also to share his destiny"[42] and Jesus told his followers what that destiny should include:

> *"Go therefore and make disciples of all nations, baptizing them in the name of the Father and of the Son and of the Holy Spirit, and teaching them to obey everything that I have commanded you. And remember, I am with you always, to the end of the age."*[43]

And so, as we are coming to understand the history of our patient (the Church), we are beginning to see how years and years of disagreement and division over proper orthodoxy have contributed to our present condition...a condition in which beliefs take priority over and above behaviors.

---

[42] John Howard Yoder, *The Politics of Jesus: Vicit Agnus Noster*, 2nd ed. (Grand Rapids, Mich.: Wm. B. Eerdmans Publishing Company, 1994), 124.
[43] Matthew 28:18-20. (NRSV)

Now it is time to ask a couple of questions:

- What adaptive behaviors have we engaged in as a way to deal with this condition?

- What has our preoccupation with beliefs over behaviors cost us in ecclesial currency?

It is to these issues we now turn.

Chapter 2 - Adaptive Strategies

Diagnostic Strategy: How do you cope with these symptoms?

Most of you reading this book have had some experience with dating in your life. Dating is the way many of us met and fell in love with our spouses, which is a good thing. But, on the road to this destination there were likely a few bumps that caused us to doubt or question our identity. Some of those bumps were likely the result of an experience similar to the following:

We have all heard the old adage that opposites attract and at some point in our dating life we probably were infatuated with someone very different from ourselves: we may even be married to one. However, at this early stage of life, we did not have the self-confidence or perhaps the sheer nerve to embrace this difference. So, in an effort to make ourselves more attractive to the object of our affections, we attempted to become a person we thought they might like better. To accomplish this, we started to like the same things they liked, dress the same way they dressed, listen to the same music they listened to, and hang out with the same people they hung out with. While this strategy may initially have had positive results, our true self is hard to keep hidden for extended periods of time, so eventually when the object of our intentions came to know the real us and understand the depth of our deception, they not only left us, but left us not knowing who we really were.

In many ways, this is the story of the current state of the Church in the West, for in our preoccupation with beliefs over and above behaviors (the *way*) we have concentrated our efforts on ways to make our beliefs more palatable to the cultural appetite, or as the dating metaphor above suggests, present ourselves in a way that is more culture-friendly so they will like us. Unfortunately, these efforts tend to backfire, leaving us alone and confused with a diminished understanding of not only who we are but without a clear understanding of what it truly means to be a follower of Christ; one that embraces the *way* and the *truth* that leads to *life*.

Now you might ask, how is the Church engaging in adaptive behaviors such as these? We engage in adaptive behaviors when we pursue more attractional strategies, strategies that exist to make us more appealing as a way to entice people to attend our church. We do this when we present ourselves as "insert current trendy catch phrase here", or create a cool web site, or redecorate, or add candles to the sanctuary, or change casual Friday to casual Sunday, or play more contemporary music, or install video projectors, or have a Halloween trick or treat event at the church, or free coffee and donuts in the lobby, or popcorn, or Jupiter jumps, or dunk tanks, or car shows or, or, or… The list goes on and on as a Church that used to ring bells to call the community together to worship is increasingly in the bells and whistles business.[44]

Some might argue these are attempts on the part of the Church to be more in tune with the culture; anything to tell people about Jesus, and there is some degree of truth concealed within that claim albeit a rather anemic one. However, even in that particular defense of our actions, we are illuminating the

---

[44] Leonard Sweet, *Nudge: Awakening Each Other to the God Who's Already There* (Colorado Springs, CO: David C. Cook, 2010), 60-61.

degree to which we lean more toward telling than doing...of believing rather than behaving.

These types of adaptive behaviors are not unlike those we observed earlier in our patient examples; they are Band-Aids rather than cures; ways in which we can give the appearance of being healthy and happy while obscuring the ecclesial dysfunction lurking just below the surface. In addition, the fact that we are even engaging in these adaptive behaviors provides evidence of the degree to which we will go to avoid actually living out a life that is true to the *way* of Jesus.

Diagnostic Question: How has this condition affected you?

As we discussed earlier, adaptive behaviors come with a cost...an *opportunity cost* and in our case they cost us in the following ways:

• We lose the opportunity to pursue healthy strategies that would serve to mitigate our further decline.

• We suffer the cultural consequences that result from our actions or lack thereof.

Truth or Consequences

Fortunately or unfortunately depending on how you choose to frame the issue, as the Church has leaned more heavily into the promoting of beliefs over and above living in a *way* that prioritizes care for the less fortunate, other organizations have come in to claim that space: primarily NPOs (non-profit organizations) and government agencies. To make matters worse, it appears we are not the least bit troubled by this situation. In fact, we may actually prefer it this way since it gives us the ability to deny our actions, or lack thereof, are having any negative cultural consequences while simultaneously allowing us to engage in beliefs based adaptive strategies.

Granted, some churches are actively involved in care for the "least of these" among us and they are to be commended for these efforts, but for the most part in Western culture, those who find themselves in need tend to seek out government programs and social service agencies rather than attempting to get help from a local church. While this strategy does give individuals access to an abundance of resources, the fact that the Church is not even considered as an option for those in need should cause us some degree of ecclesial concern.

Another development that should possibly concern us even more is how some churches are attempting to fulfill their obligation to their community by providing space within their facilities for the offices of social service agencies. On one hand this might seem like a great idea, but what is the underlying message of this strategy? Is it that the church itself is not capable or perhaps willing to commit to meeting the needs of the people they are called to serve? Or, are the needs just too great for the local church and the best they can do is direct people to the existing catalog of social services and governmental agencies? Either way, one thing it makes perfectly clear is the boundary between church and state: if you need help, seek out a social service agency, but if you need counseling on spiritual issues (what to believe), the Church is here for you.

As the Church is increasingly known as the promoter of beliefs over and above being known as a people who live in the *way* of Jesus, it is losing the foundation on which to stand for those beliefs. This footing is especially precarious in a postmodern age where a greater emphasis is placed on *experiential truth* over and above *propositional truth*.

Postmoderns want to experience truth, to see a "people who live out the gospel in wholesome, authentic, and healing relationships."[45] If they see a church whose truths are disconnected from the enacting of those truths, then those truths are left without authority. Consequently, rather than align themselves with an institution they view as invalid, postmoderns are in greater and greater numbers choosing a religious affiliation of "none."

> "In the last five years alone, the unaffiliated have increased from just over 15% to just under 20% of all U.S. adults. Their ranks now include more than 13 million self-described atheists and agnostics (nearly 6% of the U.S. public), as well as nearly 33 million people who say they have no particular religious affiliation (14%)."[46]

---

[45] Stanley J. Grenz, *A Primer On Postmodernism* (Grand Rapids, Mich.: Wm. B. Eerdmans Publishing Company, 1996), 169.
[46] Pew Research / Religion and Public Life Project. http://www.pewforum.org/2012/10/09/nones-on-the-rise

In Canada, those who claim no affiliation with religion has risen from 4% in 1972 to 24% in 2011[1], and in Australia, the number of those reporting to have no religious affiliation has risen from "one in 250 in 1911 to more than one in five in 2011." [2] This is a not just a local phenomenon but something we are seeing throughout the West.

[1] http://www.pewforum.org/2013/06/27/canadas-changing-religious-landscape/

As the number of those with no religious affiliation continues to rise, the Church finds itself increasingly diminished in its ability to influence the culture. For an example of this we need only consider the current political climate in which alignment with a particular religious perspective is a way others tend to invalidate that position and exclude that person from the conversation.

However, this is not the only consequence to declining religious affiliation we must confront for as government and social service agencies expand their health care services, they are increasingly providing care in ways that do not align with many of the values the Church tends to embrace. To better understand this we need look no further than the ever-contentious Roe v. Wade. This controversial legal decision was perhaps the first shot across the bow of the Church from a culture that wanted to let us know in no uncertain terms things are different now. Consequently, many churches have engaged in a variety of attempts to overturn this controversial decision in the courts of the land. What perhaps went unnoticed in this strategy was how the culture had migrated issues of morality to the court system, away and apart from the institution (the Church) that had presided over these issues for centuries.

In its purest form, one could argue this was an attempt by the Church to defend its beliefs through whatever means necessary. However, many would interpret these actions as the Church's attempt to legislate and therein enforce its beliefs upon a culture that increasingly wanted no part of it.

---

[2] http://www.heraldsun.com.au/news/victoria/almost-five-million-australians-says-they-have-no-religious-beliefs/story-fni0fit3-1226791614342?nk=2546604f8f3478af64ee50fc65d31131

This legal strategy has contributed to Christians being referred to as "religious zealots, peddlers of coercion, religious nuts, self-proclaimed moral leaders, fanatics, extremists, moral zealots, fear brokers, right-wing homophobes etc."[47] However, as Christians we have not been those who turn the other cheek[48] to these assertions for we have hurled equally egregious accusations at those who oppose us such as "arrogant and self-righteous, militant, deceitful, treacherous, masters of deceit, intellectual barbarians, amoral, anti-Christian, a godless liberal philosophy, ruthless, insidious, [and] the forces of the anti-Christ."[49]

This strife and division between Church and culture has risen to such a fevered pitch that many consider us to be in the midst of a full-blown culture war; one that will ultimately determine "not who is right but who is left."[50]

While much can be made about the increasing rate of decline Christianity experienced post Enlightenment, it could be argued that the predicament in which the Church now finds itself in the Western world was actually fueled by an event near and dear to Protestants: the Reformation.

The Reformation, as we will remember, is the point in history when the one and true Church of the day cracked open and became a variety of churches with competing truth claims, effectively ending more than 1000 years of Christianity serving as the shared intellectual basis for life in the Latin West.[51] As a

---

[47] James Davison Hunter, *Culture Wars: The Struggle to Define America* (New York: BasicBooks, 1991), 144.
[48] Matthew 5:39, Luke 6:29.
[49] Hunter, *Culture Wars*, 144-145.
[50] Ibid., 136.
[51] Gregory, *The Unintended Reformation*, 45.

consequence, rather than a united Church attempting to defend or deflect an ideological onslaught from the forces of humanism and scholasticism, the Church instead brought to bear the full weight of its intellectual capacities against itself in a maelstrom of theological controversy.[52] The Enlightenment further contributed to the decline of the Church by suggesting scientific ways in which the world could understand itself "that did not depend on any contested Christian doctrine."[53]

It wasn't long until this divided kingdom was soon to take another blow, as a collection of modern thinkers began to dismantle and deconstruct not only the idea that Jesus was the truth, but that an ultimate truth even existed.

People such as Hobbes, Rousseau, Kant, Schopenhaur, Marx, Darwin, and Niezsche all questioned the truth that had inspired humanity for thousands of years.

> "Before Darwin, the orderliness of nature and its wonders, from the eye of a bird to the brain of a human, called for a grand designer who created the world."[54]

With the arrival of Darwin's book "On the Origin of the Species", natural selection entered the public square and attempted to demote and dislodge God from His position of prominence. Friedrich Nietzsche even carried it a step further when he dared to proclaim that God was dead, no longer playing a "vital role in our culture."[55]

---

[52] Ibid.
[53] Ibid., 47.
[54] Louis P. Pojman, *Who Are We?: Theories of Human Nature* (New York: Oxford University Press, USA, 2005), 205.
[55] Ibid., 186.

Their thinking was fueled by enlightenment revelations as they believed only verifiable and repeatable scientific results had the intellectual weight necessary to approach the realm of truth. Unfortunately, this scientific approach carries with it negative consequences: scientific truth only retains authority until a new and better truth emerges. Consequently, doubt and uncertainty hang like dark clouds over all these transient truths while "the truth" gets demoted to just one of many truths competing for prominence on the political landscape.

As this politics of truth continues to gain prominence, "institutions such as popular and higher education, philanthropy, science, the arts, and even the family understand their identity and function according to what the state does or does not permit."[56] Consequently, each and every variant of the political spectrum (including the Church) attempts to advance their moral foundation in the marketplace of ideas through very post-enlightenment means…through superior reasoning or the most rational argument. However, this cultural test of wills is frustrated due to the fact the positions of both sides are crafted under quite different rules of logic and moral judgment which results in everyone speaking or shouting in languages the other cannot understand.[57]

The Church has embraced the political solution to such a degree that it has caused some to suggest "the dominant public witness of the Christian churches in America since the early 1980s has been a political witness."[58] This should cause us

---

[56] James Davison Hunter, *To Change the World: the Irony, Tragedy, and Possibility of Christianity in the Late Modern World* (New York: Oxford University Press, USA, 2010), 103.
[57] Hunter, *Culture Wars*, 250.
[58] Hunter, *To Change the World*, 12.

some degree of concern in that it lies in glaring contrast to the image of the early church being known as the Church of the *way*.

The adaptive behavior of political evangelism also carries with it certain negative consequences. Consider the following illustration. Assume an individual runs for political office promoting their strong Christian convictions as a reason to support their candidacy. Promoting oneself as a Christian candidate is usually code: it is a way to transmit the message to the voting populace that the candidate supports certain issues without actually having to insert those issues into the debate. But now suppose this politician (now elected) takes a stance that is counter to your beliefs. Since he ran for office stating he would let his Christian faith inspire his actions, those with whom he now disagrees are hard pressed to separate his Christianity from his political position. As a result, Christianity takes a hit along with the politician while seemingly providing evidence to support continued efforts to separate church and state. This association gets even more heated as thoughtful and committed Christians on both sides of some of our country's most contentious issues ravage the political terrain while attempting to claim the theological high ground.

In recent history, political action groups arose which claimed to be the defenders of the Christian faith such as Jerry Falwell's Moral Majority, James Dobson's Focus on the Family, and Pat Robertson's Christian Coalition etc. Recognizing the decline of Christian influence in the U.S., their self-appointed task was to "increase the number of Christians working in the realm of law and public policy at all levels of government and, short of that to mobilize popular indignation to pressure politicians to support the policies and laws compatible with [their version of] Christian principles."[59] While most of these organizations are currently on life support, others are rising to take their place and will likely continue engaging in political strategies that increase ideological divides rather that build bridges for mutual understanding.

Christian political engagement is further fueled by the cohabitation of American Exceptionalism with the idea that America is a Christian nation. Those in this particular camp see America as a country founded on Christian principles…a beacon on a hill whose purpose and responsibility is to spread its particular brand of Christian democracy throughout the world. To those with this understanding, a diminishing Christian influence in the political theater is a failure of America to live up to its pre-ordained role in the world.

Without attempting to engage the truth or fiction of this position, we need only remember the historical examples where the Church became collateral damage in many a marriage between the Church and ruling powers in history. While the Church can serve to strengthen a government in need of such strength, once that government is able to stand on its own feet, the role of the Church is consequently diminished, as morality and principle tend to get in the way of economic prosperity and the quest for power.

For another example of the negative consequences associated with attempting to enforce morality upon a somewhat rebellious populace, we can refer to Paul's assessment of the Law of the Hebrew Bible: *"All that passing laws*

---

[59] Hunter, *To Change the World*, 13.

against sin did was produce more lawbreakers;"[60] so much for trying to legislate morality into existence.

To underscore what Paul is saying here, let's pause for a moment and consider some consequential realities:

- Have laws against murder ended murders?

- Have laws against rape or sexual abuse put an end to those behaviors?

- Do most people obey speed limits?

- Have laws against marijuana and other drugs eliminated the market for such things?

The list could go on and on as our prisons continue to fill with those unlucky enough to be caught in their act of law breaking. This situation points to what Paul knew, and the Gospel proclaims, the Law or a cornucopia of laws will not change behaviors or more importantly get to the root of the issue, for the issue is the condition of the human heart.

Perhaps the most insidious consequence of attempting to legislate Christian behaviors onto an unwilling populace lies in how this strategy seems to place Christian beliefs and ultimately God in a place that is secondary to the government and politics. When the Church is in need of validation through the political process, it ceases to be the manifestation of Christ on this earth and instead confirms its location on the road to cultural irrelevance. I suggest our preoccupation with politics in Christianity is possibly one of the most damaging strategies in which we as the Church have engaged in modern history. In

---

[60] Romans 5:20. (MSG)

fact, it is not out of line to suggest "contemporary Christian understandings of power and politics are a very large part of what has made contemporary Christianity in America appalling, irrelevant, and ineffective - part and parcel of the worst elements of our late-modern culture today, rather than a healthy alternative to it."[61]

Thus, the Church must never place itself in the position from which it seeks validation through the political strategies of the world, for the more it attempts to influence or enforce its values or morals upon an unwilling populace, the more it furnishes evidence that it has "become a thing of this world."[62] For the Church is not a thing of the world existing "peripheral to the world; the world is peripheral to the church. The church is Christ's body, in which he speaks and acts, by which he fills everything with his presence."[63] And, until the Church inhabits a position from which we inspire the world...a terrain in which our behaviors match our beliefs...the influence of our schizophrenic church will continue to decline.

Those are pretty strong words, but if you are a parent or were ever a child, think back to how children typically respond to rules that attempt to restrict behaviors. Rules were followed to the degree the child accepted the authority of the parent. Without a recognition of that authority, the rule was nothing more than an idle proclamation of parental preference and would typically result in the child or teenager attempting to hide the behavior from the parent while doing it anyway. However, if the child or teen loved the parent and thereby

---

[61] Hunter, *To Change the World*, 95.
[62] Walter Rauschenbusch, *The Righteousness of the Kingdom* (Nashville: Abingdon Press, rpr. 1968), pp. 92-93.
[63] Ephesians 1:23. (MSG)

accepted their authority over the child, the threat of punishment was not nearly as compelling as the thought of letting the parent down or somehow falling short of either parental expectations or the child's idea of self.

One of the great ironies we tend to overlook as the Church pursues influence via political means arises from the fact God already reigns over and above any and all political institutions. The Church does not exist to serve the state and the Church does not need the validation of the state to feel good about itself. In fact, if the Church finds itself in a position in which the state defers power to the Church, we should probably throw in the towel and acknowledge that we are no longer the representatives of a savior crucified 2000 years ago, but instead are just another agency working alongside the state helping to improve the lives of a subjugated populace.

The existence of the Church as a global body of faith stands as a "sign that God, not nations, rule this world."[64] The Church can never exist as an equal partner to the world's political systems for "the world knows not the God we find in scripture."[65] As such, strategies by the Church that attempt to engage and solve the challenges of our time in partnership with the world are destined to fail, for one can not partner with that which one does not know.

Oftentimes in these types of discussions honest and faithful Christians suggest it is their Christian duty to engage the culture through political means. This raises a question: if we claim our politics are inspired by our efforts to engage the

---

[64] Stanley Hauerwas, *A Community of Character: Toward a Constructive Christian Social Ethic* (Notre Dame: University of Notre Dame Press, 1991), 109-110.
[65] Ibid., 68.

culture in a Christian way, just how political was Jesus? It is to this issue we now turn.

The Politics of Jesus

If we are to attempt to answer the question "Was Jesus political?" with any integrity, we must answer in a paradoxical way (which seems to happen a lot when we talk about Jesus). The answer is *yes* and *no*. Yes, Jesus was quite political, but not in the manner in which we tend to think about politics. First let's look at the "no" side of the ledger.

From what we read of Jesus in the Gospels, he appears unconcerned with the politics of this world. We read nothing of Jesus encouraging his disciples to work to influence or infiltrate the political structures of the day, nor any proclamations referencing his desire to do that in the future. Instead Jesus was about people irrespective of their political leanings or place in the social hierarchy. If anything, Jesus seemed more interested in the disenfranchised… those living at the fringes of society over and above those whose position placed them in a higher strata of social and political hierarchies of the day. The Pharisees, no doubt aware of this, tried to lure Jesus into a position that would place Him on the wrong side of the reigning political/legal system by asking him a trick question concerning whether it is lawful to pay taxes to Caesar:

> *"Then the Pharisees went and plotted to entrap him in what he said. So they sent their disciples to him, along with the Herodians, saying, 'Teacher, we know that you are sincere, and teach the way of God in accordance with truth, and show deference to no one; for you do not regard people with partiality. Tell us, then, what you*

think. Is it lawful to pay taxes to the emperor, or not?' But Jesus, aware of their malice, said, 'Why are you putting me to the test, you hypocrites? Show me the coin used for the tax.' And they brought him a denarius. Then he said to them, 'Whose head is this, and whose title?' They answered, 'The emperor's.' Then he said to them, 'Give therefore to the emperor the things that are the emperor's, and to God the things that are God's.'"[66]

In his answer, Jesus not only averted their attempt to entrap him, but also made very clear the things of God and the things of man are distinct and separate. He said to give to the earthly ruler what is rightly his and give to God the things that are sovereignly God's. Jesus did not say the people should resist the payment of taxes that are potentially deemed too high or injurious. He did not say rather than pay the taxes Caesar demanded, they should seek to have those taxes reduced to a more agreeable and acceptable level. And, he did not say that as Jews they should create and print a currency of their own so they could avoid giving Caesar his due. No. Jesus answered very simply, there are two kingdoms…one of this world and one of God…do not confuse the two. Jesus' lack of concern for a tax system, which arguably was burdensome for the population, gives us a strong indication Jesus was not interested in modifying, infiltrating, or changing the world's system through the politics of this world.

There is quite a bit more weight on the "yes" side of the ledger as relates to the politics of Jesus but not in terms of earthly politics. As background, Israel lived with an expectation of a Messianic king. It was a story rooted in their history and one, which reverberates throughout the pages of their sacred

---

[66] Matthew 22:15.

texts. They had heard these stories since childhood and in these stories it would be hard to overlook a recurring theme: "the wicked tyrant oppressing God's people, the noble and heroic leader risking all, fighting the key battle, cleansing the Temple, and setting Israel free to follow God and his law once more. This was the story of Moses, Egypt, and the Exodus. It was the story of David, Solomon, the Philistines, and the Temple. It was the story of Babylon overthrown, of return from exile."[67] And it was a story many expected to be repeated once again.

Much is written on this topic and if you are interested in digging deeper into the Messianic expectation of Israel, there are many books that can indulge your curiosity. However, here we will provide a brief overview of some Biblical indicators that do indeed make Israel's expectation of a promised Messiah apparent.

A Miraculous Birth

We join the story at the point of an angelic announcement to an unsuspecting young girl of Nazareth:

> *"Do not be afraid, Mary, for you have found favor with God. And now, you will conceive in your womb and bear a son, and you will name him Jesus. He will be great, and will be called the Son of the Most High, and the Lord God will give to him the throne of his ancestor David. He will reign over the house of Jacob forever, and of his kingdom there will be no end."*[68]

---

[67] N. T. Wright, *Simply Jesus: Who He Was, What He Did, Why It Matters* (New York: HarperOne, 2011), 107.
[68] Luke 1:30-33.

With this announcement, Mary learns her son of special circumstance would be great, would be the Son of God, would occupy the throne of King David, and oversee a kingdom of which there would be no end. We can surmise Mary did not see this coming, and yet here is her response:

> "Here am I, the servant of the Lord; let it be with me according to your word."[69]

Shortly thereafter, Mary goes to visit her cousin Elizabeth who was expecting her own miraculous child.[70] Upon Mary's entrance into the room, Elizabeth's child jumped within her[71] prompting Elizabeth to greet Mary in what was likely an unexpected manner:

> "Blessed are you among women, and blessed is the fruit of your womb. And why has this happened to me, that the mother of my Lord comes to me?"[72]

"The mother of my Lord" is pretty strong language. It is not hard to imagine the excitement of a young girl, pregnant by unusual means receiving a confirmation of something known only to her and her somewhat skeptical fiancée Joseph. Joseph of course received confirmation[73] of the identity of Mary's child and set out to protect her and the child from the suspicion and ridicule that no doubt would come. Upon the birth of their son Jesus, shepherds[74] and wise men[75] also confirmed the identity of this newborn king.

---

[69] Luke 1:38.
[70] Luke 1:39-45.
[71] Luke 1:41.
[72] Luke 1:41-42.
[73] Matthew 1:20.
[74] Luke 3:20-22.
[75] Matthew 2:2.

We can also look to Herod for evidence to support the expectation of a Messiah for when the wise men arrived asking Herod where they could find this newborn king; Herod did not ask what they were talking about nor question the legitimacy of their question. Instead he instructed the wise men to let him know where they found the child so that he could come and worship him as well.[76] Herod must have felt threatened by this new king in that when the wise men did not return to identify the location of this child king, Herod sought out "all the chief priests and scribes of the people"[77] to inquire where the scriptures indicated the Messiah would be born.[78] Herod then attempted to eliminate the possibility of any young male child in that region growing to challenge his authority.[79]

Another Miraculous Birth

John the Baptist played a distinctive role in the arrival of the coming Messiah for John's entrance into the world was also accompanied by some rather miraculous events as angels announced his arrival prior to his birth:

> *"You will have joy and gladness, and many will rejoice at his birth, for he will be great in the sight of the Lord. He must never drink wine or strong drink; even before his birth he will be filled with the Holy Spirit. He will turn many of the people of Israel to the Lord their God. With the spirit and power of Elijah he will go before him, to turn the hearts of parents to their children, and the*

---

[76] Matthew 2:8.
[77] Matthew 2:4
[78] Matthew 2:4.
[79] Matthew 2:16

disobedient to the wisdom of the righteous, to make ready a people prepared for the Lord."[80]

John's task was to get the people ready for the arrival of the coming Messiah. In doing so, John preached a baptism of repentance with singular style and enthusiasm informing people the time had come to *"Repent, for the kingdom of heaven is near."*[81] John also made quite clear he was not the chosen one; he was only a supporting character on this stage:

"I baptize you with water for repentance, but one who is more powerful than I is coming after me; I am not worthy to carry his sandals. He will baptize you with the Holy Spirit and fire."[82]

Later, John the Baptist even baptized Jesus in spite of John's reluctance to do so. And, at the moment of this baptism something amazing happened; the Holy Spirit in the form of something like a dove descended upon Jesus and a voice was heard that echoed throughout eternity:

"This is my Son, the Beloved, with whom I am well pleased."[83]

As word reached John concerning the miraculous things happening around Jesus, John sent his disciples to ask Jesus a question:

"Are you the one who is to come, or are we to wait for another?"[84]

His question is beautiful in its simplicity and yet revealing in its content. Are you the one... the Messiah the scriptures promised would come, or should we continue waiting and

---

[80] Luke 1:14-17.
[81] Matthew 3:2. (NIV)
[82] Matthew 3:11, Mark 1:7-8, Luke 3:16, John 1:26.
[83] Matthew 3:17, Mark 1:11, Luke 3:22.
[84] Matthew 11:3.

looking for another? Jesus answered as Jesus does[85] but the message was loud and clear…I am.

Jesus' Entry into Jerusalem

Upon Jesus' arrival in Jerusalem, what are the people saying…what message floats above the buzz of the crowd? It is something Jesus seems now willing to acknowledge for He tells his disciples *"Tell the daughter of Zion, Look, your king is coming to you, humble, and mounted on a donkey, and on a colt, the foal of a donkey."*[86]

Then, as Jesus begins his approach into Jerusalem on the back of this lowly pack animal *"the whole multitude of the disciples began to praise God joyfully with a loud voice for all the deeds of power that they had seen, saying, 'Blessed is the king who comes in the name of the Lord! Peace in heaven, and glory in the highest heaven!'"*[87] Blessed be the "king"…not the prophet… not the great teacher…but the king. And yet, Jesus was not to be the kind of king they were expecting.

Shortly thereafter, the religious leaders had Jesus arrested and taken before Pilate in hopes of having him executed to put an end to their "Jesus" problem. Pilate, the ruling representative of Rome, had a few questions for Jesus:

"'Are you the King of the Jews?' Jesus answered, 'Do you ask this on your own, or did others tell you about me?' Pilate replied, 'I am not a Jew, am I? Your own nation and the chief priests have

---

[85] Matthew 11:3-6, John 7:22-23.
[86] Matthew 21:5, Mark 11:3, Luke 19:31.
[87] Luke 19:37-38, Matthew 21:9, Mark11:9-10. John 12:13.

handed you over to me. What have you done?' Jesus answered, 'My kingdom is not from this world. If my kingdom were from this world, my followers would be fighting to keep me from being handed over to the Jews. But as it is, my kingdom is not from here.' Pilate asked him, 'So you are a king?' Jesus answered, 'You say that I am a king. For this I was born, and for this I came into the world, to testify to the truth. Everyone who belongs to the truth listens to my voice.'"[88]

It is in this response that we find our answer: Jesus was born to be a king, not a worldly king, but a king of a new world, a world that exists in contrast to this earthy world.

The Bible tells us even Satan was aware of Jesus' kingship for we have an example of Satan attempting to lure Jesus away from his purpose, in part, with the promise of another kingdom. The story records three attempts by Satan to detach Jesus from his purpose, the third of which was a political temptation…the opportunity to oversee and control the politics of the world:

"Again, the devil took him to a very high mountain and showed him all the kingdoms of the world and their splendor; and he said to him, 'All these I will give you, if you will fall down and worship me.' Jesus said to him, 'Away with you, Satan! for it is written, Worship the Lord your God, and serve only him.'"[89]

Without going too deep into the subtext here, Jesus was offered the chance to control worldly politics and reign over worldly kingdoms if he would deny God: Jesus did not, for he was already the king of another kingdom.

---

[88] John 18:33-37.
[89] Matthew 4:8-10.

So, was Jesus political?

The answer is *no* and *yes*... paradoxical as Jesus typically is.

Jesus was not political in the sense we try to make him political today through our efforts to claim Christian nation status or inject Christian ideals into the political marketplace. Instead Jesus' politics were directed toward the establishment of a new kingdom over and above our earthly kingdoms...a kingdom in which God rules and reigns and in which the kingdom of Heaven is lived out now and forever. His purpose was not to gain approval or have his principles legitimated through legal discourse, but instead was to establish the kingdom: a shining light on a hill illuminating all the earth.

We can say Jesus was political in the sense he was a king, he just wasn't the kind of king the Israelites were expecting. Instead "Jesus was, in his divinely mandated (i.e., promised, anointed, messianic) prophethood, priesthood, and kingship, the bearer of a new possibility of human, social, and therefore political relationships."[90] "Instead of hanging His hopes and dreams on the course of a country, He hung it all on a cross"[91] as Jesus established his kingdom in a new geography...the geography of the human heart. As such, "Jesus didn't choose the primacy of the powers of religion/politics or the powers of the individual; He chose a third way - His indwelling presence experienced and displayed through a community of followers who embody the kingdom of God in their corporate life together:"[92] in other words, a new politics, one that is lived out

---

[90] Hunter, *Culture Wars*, 52.
[91] Jonathan Merritt, *A Faith of Our Own: Following Jesus Beyond the Culture Wars* (New York: FaithWords, 2012), 82.
[92] Leonard Sweet and Frank Viola, *Jesus: a Theography* (Nashville, Tenn.: Thomas Nelson, 2012), 119.

by a group of people who live in a certain *way*, a *way* that manifests this new kingdom reality on earth...as it is in heaven. [93]

The Question

In our patient examples discussed earlier, we observed how adaptive behaviors are seen as successful up to the point where they no longer are...up to the point where the patient either falls on their face due to exhaustion or finally acknowledges the reality that they have a problem and the way they have been dealing with it just isn't working anymore.

Assuming we are willing to take a serious look at the current condition of our Church, we need to be asking ourselves some questions:

• Are we happy with the location our church currently occupies in the cultural landscape?

• Are we comfortable with what appears to be our current trajectory?

• Do we feel like our church is a manifestation of the church God intended?

If the answers to these questions arouse even the slightest degree of concern on our parts for our Church, we have a decision to make: do we accept the current state of our Church as its *new normal* and direct our efforts toward keeping it comfortable as it continues on this downward trajectory?

---

[93] Matthew 6:10.

Or, do we have the courage to pursue *a new normal*... *a new normal* in which the Church of our Lord...the Body of Christ... returns to a spiritual geography on which the Church does more than just survive, but thrives in a way that manifests the love of Jesus to a culture desperate to see this faith in action?

Let's assume our answer to this second question is yes; we do want to pursue the higher road that leads to a new normal we can live with. Then, the next step in our diagnostic investigation is to do a little testing on the patient (the Church) to see if we can uncover the primary cause of our declining condition.

Part 2 – Diagnostic Testing

Chapter 3 – Test Results

Diagnostic Strategy: Let's Run A Few Tests.

One of the primary ways a diagnostician can uncover or confirm the cause of a dis-ease or dis-function is to perform a series of tests. These tests can be as simple as taking one's temperature, looking in the throat, and listening to the lungs or heart through a stethoscope. However, in more complicated diagnoses, a series of tests are likely to be performed in an effort to confirm or deny the existence of a particular condition. This strategy is not exclusive to the medical community.

As it turns out, I am getting back to writing today after concluding a visit to our home by a plumber. Our toilet was leaking around its base…a relatively simple thing to fix if you are so inclined and have the appropriate tools. However, I abandoned efforts to engage in home plumbing activities years ago since I really had no idea what I was doing. The time I invested in plumbing repairs typically required I make multiple trips to the hardware store to get things I didn't know I needed on the previous trip…or perhaps to get a replacement for something I had broken in my misdirected efforts. So, today rather than lose the opportunity to make forward progress on this book, I just called the plumber.

However, even for this rather simple repair, the plumber went through a bit of diagnostics before confirming the problem:

- How much was leaking?
- Was the toilet still draining?

• Is it secure to the floor? Etc.

• Sounds like the wax seal. I should be out of here in about an hour.

Even in something as simple as a toilet, a bit of diagnostic evaluation is a good thing. So, to help us uncover the primary cause of our ecclesial difficulties, let's run a little test.

Our need to perform diagnostic testing on our patient (the Church) is fulfilled through the 10 Things research mentioned earlier. As you will remember from the prologue, this research consisted of the creation of an online forum where individuals could vent their disapproval for the Church or Christians. The tenthingsproject.com included tenthingsihateaboutchurch.com and tenthingsihageaboutchristians.com. Both of these sites presented no pre-determined categories in which to contribute, just 10 slots in which the contributors could post those 10 things that most bothered them about the Church or Christians.

The project was in active research mode for 6 months and logged 825 contributions. Contributors were from all over the country and from a wide variety of age groups. While its initial purpose was to take the pulse and listen to the heart of non-Christians, surprisingly 86% of the contributors were actually Christians and 8% of those were church staff members.

Categories

I was able to place the contributions into four basic categories with of course exceptions for those that were beyond explanation. I called these categories *behaviors*, *perceptions*, *beliefs* and *practices*. Eventually it became obvious these four categories were really two primary categories related to *behaviors* and *beliefs* with the addition of a category for *miscellaneous* and one for those who in spite of the title of the collection site chose to express their affection for both their fellow Christians and their Church. And so, out of respect for their efforts, there is a *love* category. In addition, the data was broken down into three demographic groups: Christians, Church Staff and Non-Christians. It is from this collection of symptoms that our diagnosis will be revealed.

Behaviors

We all know what a behavior is but to make sure we are all on the same page let's go with the definition from the Oxford American Dictionary: "the way in which one acts or conducts oneself, especially toward others." To that end, this category will concern itself with the behaviors associated with Christians and how they conduct themselves with one another and the world.

Beliefs

Beliefs (for our purposes) are defined as those ideologies concerned with the doctrine or truths of the Church and Christianity, or as the Oxford American Dictionary puts it; "religious convictions."

The Test Results on Christians

Now let's dig into the data, look at how it lays out in a graphic format, and then discuss some of what the results tell us. The following chart illustrates a breakdown of the data contributed to *Ten Things I Hate About Christians* web site. The vertical axis indicates the percentage of contributions in a particular category and the horizontal axis identifies the 4 categories.

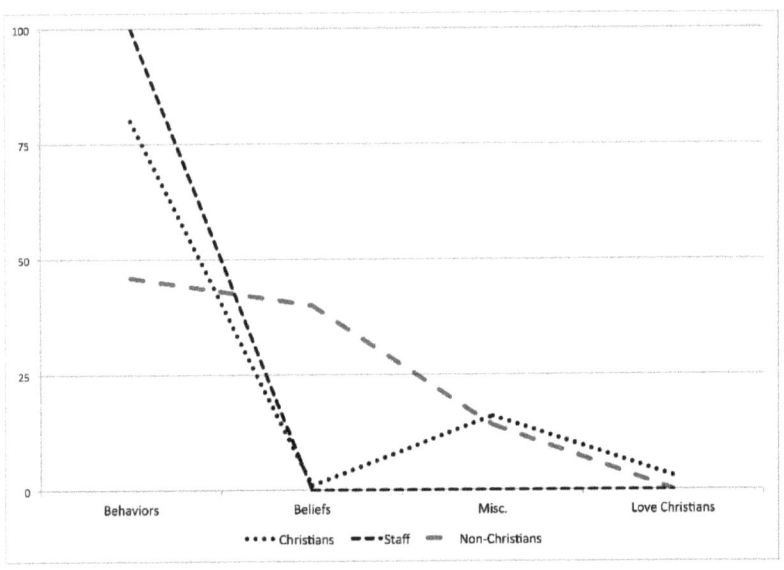

Behaviors of Christians

According to the research, each of our three demographic groups agrees in that they share a common disdain for the behavior of Christians. If we drill down in the data further, we see the comments cluster around the following categories: hypocrisy, self-interest, judgmental attitude, lack of understanding, ineffectiveness, club mentality, closed minded attitude, gossip, worldly, misunderstanding of beliefs, lack of love, and a catch all category of miscellaneous for both the insightful and the snarky. Here is a selection of some of the comments. Remember, these comments should be considered under the question: What are 10 things you hate about Christians?

Christians on the Behavior of Christians

- *"Christians say they believe in God and walk in his ways and their attitudes show differently."*
- *"Christians who seek their own glory rather than God's."*
- *"They are the first to criticize and the last to take criticism."*
- *"Lack of authenticity. Acting like all is well when it is not."*
- *"Most worship the preacher and other things instead of God."*
- *"They set bad examples for their children to follow and do not even know it."*
- *"People who are more interested in making the church a social club instead of an extension of God's love."*
- *"You have to meet their standards before they will be friends with you."*
- *"Christians should be focused on God but the world sees Christians focused on the same things they are: concerts, sporting events, fashions, and other things of false value."*
- *"People who think just because they go to church on Sunday, sing a few songs, and listen to the pastor, they think this makes them a Christian."*
- *"Pastors feel the need to be hip, which for most is something they are not."*
- *"Beaten down non-victorious lives"*
- *"Detachment from the real world"*
- *"Forgot how to have fun."*
- *"Jesus is lost in the crowd."*

Church Staff on the Behavior of Christians
- *"They all have answers but none of the fruit."*
- *"Having only Christian friends...being elitist or exclusive."*
- *"Leaving their faith for Sundays"*
- *"Lack of knowledge of what they actually believe."*
- *"TBN"*
- *"Christianese"*
- *"I hate that pastors are too afraid of losing people to speak the truth."*
- *"Ignorant of global issues...Darfur, water, orphans, AIDS, poverty, genocide, hunger, education, slavery, children soldiers..."*
- *"The more mystical they are the more spiritual and the more spiritual the deeper they know God. Yet none are hanging out under the interstate bridges with the homeless."*
- *"I hate that the sign of successful ministry is large numbers of people."*
- *"I hate when worship is about the quality of music, nobody sees that most worship music is about us rather than about God."*
- *"I hate that we don't teach people about theology, but rather give them self-help sermons."*
- *"I hate having to market Jesus."*
- *"I hate that the church has become about convenience."*
- *"I hate that Jesus has become a business."*

Non-Christians on the Behavior of Christians
- *"Your obsession about pushing your religion on non-Christians all over the world. This site is no exception... In the end you want to 'share' Jesus with everyone in hopes of conversion. Why not just let people be."*
- *"They don't respect other's beliefs."*
- *"They are PUSHY!! If I wanted to be in your church, I would have joined on my own.*
- *"Refusing to socialize with people out side of their faith."*

- *"Stop preaching love and tolerance, and practicing hate and intolerance."*
- *"Christians are hypocrites and follow a fairy story. They are turning the world to shit by their lack of vision."*
- *"The I'm better than you because I'm Christian."*
- *"They don't accept gays."*
- *"Screw others over all week then ask for forgiveness one hour on Sunday and believe it."*
- *"Most don't even know their own Christian history."*
- *"Lemmings"*
- *"Most are hypocrites."*
- *"How a lot of them seem to be brainwashed, I'm not saying all, but really, try thinking for yourself."*

Beliefs of Christians

Christians on the Beliefs of Christians

We should probably not be surprised Christians typically do not have a problem with the beliefs of their faith. After all, it was belief and trusting in the beliefs of that faith that likely prompted them to accept Christianity in the first place.

Church Staff on the Beliefs of Christians

There were no comments that could be categorized as church staff members having a problem with the theology or beliefs of the church. Again, this is understandable since they have dedicated their lives to living in and promoting those beliefs.

Non-Christians on the Beliefs of Christians

The beliefs category for non-Christians is an area in which we see quite a difference arise. The non-Christians make such comments as:
- *"Vatican tax-free billions in assets."*
- *"The fact that they have to have blind 'faith.'"*
- *"Most have weights and balances regarding which sins are worse than others."*
- *"Many Christians put blind faith in the government to couple with their blind faith in God. There's nothing wrong with having faith. But there's something wrong with having faith without knowledge, wisdom, and insight."*
- *"Christians believe the bible is historical fact."*
- *"Despite physical proof of evolution and millions of years of life believe in creation in 6 days."*
- *"All based on 2000 year old book of fables translated and rewritten countless times."*
- *"Creationism"*
- *"They have blind, irrational faith in something so obviously false, not to mention ridiculous!"*
- *"Think they are superior to other religions."*
- *"They don't believe in evolution. How can you be so stupid?"*

These criticisms are pretty specific and seem to run counter to those who suggest that Christianity has an *image* problem or that non-believers love Jesus and just not the church. Some of them even get pretty personal calling Christians *stupid, blind* and *irrational… basing their lives on fables and ancient books…as a people worthy to be mocked.* These comments stand in striking opposition to those who propose the pathway to successful outreach and church growth is found in arching our presentation of the Gospel toward more culturally accepted expressions. These comments instead tend to suggest no matter how we present our message, non-Christians are not interested because they view us with a certain disdain and therefore diminish whatever we have to say, irrespective of how it is presented.

Miscellaneous

This is the place for all those comments that just did not seem to fit neatly into any category. They varied from the insightful to the ranting's of someone whose comments were unprintable. Below is a sampling.

Miscellaneous Christian
- *"How does the saying go? No one cares how much you know until they know how much you care."*
- *"I love this site!"*
- *"Its not that the church thinks it knows everything but the people who attend who couldn't imagine that they are wrong and then write on this board..."*

Miscellaneous Church Staff
No comments.

Miscellaneous Non-Christian
The last one in this category is my personal favorite.
- *"They think they have the 'only' religion. I don't study the origins of religion because I like to keep an open mind but I know they're wrong."*
- *"Church should be about forgiveness and hope. Too much guilt!"*
- *"I know more about what their bible says than they do. When I ask them questions about things I've read, they don't even know what I'm talking about."*

- *"Christian rock"*
- *"Bibles as birthday presents"*
- *"They are so closed minded. They think they have all the answers. I'd rather have an open mind and just believe what my professor told me."* (Can this be for real?)

Love Christians

Now I know the site was designed to be a collection point for complaints, however there were a few comments (3) that swam upstream by declaring their love for Christians. Rather than just lump them into the miscellaneous category, they get acknowledged here. Notably, all such comments came from fellow Christians…no Church staff members or non-Christians.

The Test Results on the Church

Next let's look at the diagnostic data for the Church in our online forum and then discuss some of what the test results tell us. The vertical axis indicates the percentage of contributions in a particular category and the horizontal axis identifies the 4 categories.

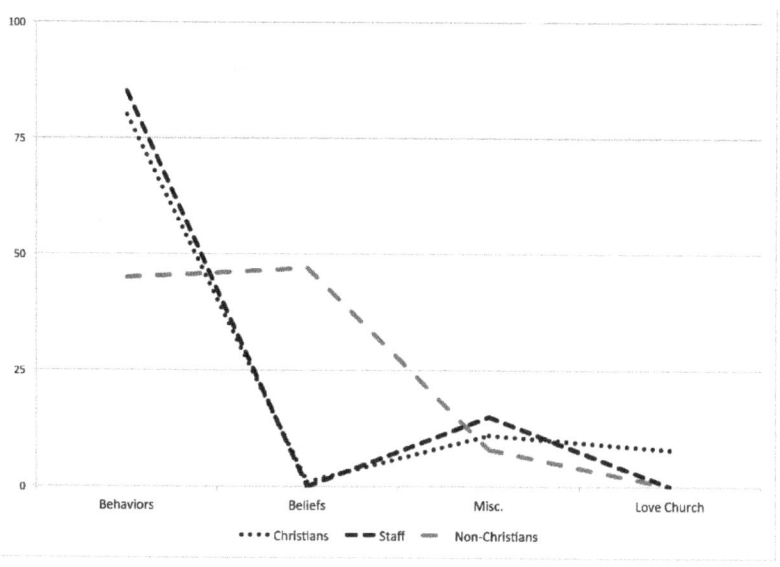

Church Behaviors

Christians on Church Behaviors

Again, we will group the comments into the categories of *behaviors, beliefs, miscellaneous,* and *love church*. But, this raises the question: isn't the behavior of a church equivalent to the behavior of the Christians in the church? It would be easy to say yes. However, these comments were made on the "church" portion of the web site, and so in an effort to maintain the integrity of the commenters' original intent, they were left in the place where they were contributed.

As such, sub-categories that emerged can be grouped into the following categories: message of the church, worship service, position of the church, mission of the church, church attempting to be relevant to the culture, direction of the church, buildings, church vs. Church, denominational system, country-club atmosphere, sub-standard practices, church experience, what determines success and of course miscellaneous. Here is a selection of the comments.

Church Behaviors
• *"Afraid of setting a high bar - don't want to run off seekers. We didn't accept Christ so all our problems would go away; in fact, it's a hard, but joyous life. We do new converts and seekers a disservice by painting a Disney picture of Christianity."*
• *"That if you aren't rich and healthy physically, then you have little faith!"*
• *"Following traditions rather than God"*
• *"People go to church to be entertained. Not convicted, encouraged, taught and sent out."*
• *"Minor things such as what type of worship music is being played takes higher priority then the message that is coming after."*
• *"Assuming more is better."*
• *"Chasm that often exists between church and culture."*
• *"Thinking that mission trips are all about making us feel better about ourselves - as long as they 'make me realize how blessed we are' and we get to shop and sightsee while we are there then it is a great experience..."*
• *"Evangelism that is done outside the context of long term relationship. Passing out tracts, street/beach evangelism where you do the sneak attack on people to 'win souls' and then you go home with no long term*

relationship, no nurture, no context for these people to understand what you are talking about and what it means long term..."
• "The church thinks that it's the coolest thing because it's so contemporary. The only problem is, the world, the people the Church is trying to reach, think it's a joke because of it."
• "When it tries to copy the world in order to 'attract' the un-churched by offering them a 'Christian' version of the world."
• "When it buys into the concept that it is a product to be sold rather than a community of people that exists"
• "Leaders who start a church with the goal in mind being to create a mega church."
• "Big buildings that cost millions of dollars and sit empty 90% of the time - when there are billions of hungry and sick people in the world."
• "That the church now pertains to you must go to a building."
• "False sense of security thinking that by attending a meeting once a week we are participating in God's church."
• "If the whole thing is for real I am positive that Jesus didn't intend for denominations"
• "Churches that think other churches suck just because they're different from their church."

Behaviors of Individuals Associated with Church
• "Leaders who don't walk the walk."
• "The behavior of those that call themselves Christians does not reflect Christ."
• "My way or no way attitude"
• "People in charge who are stuck in their ways"
• "People assume Jesus would do church exactly the way they do church"
• "Backstabbing"
• "There is no real sincerity or concern for one another in the church"
• "People hung up on man made rules"

- *"Trying to 'be real,' which seems to be just another way of covering up who we really are."*
- *"People who come to church to obtain what THEY want, as opposed seeking what GOD wants."*
- *"Instead of talking about people, why not help them? (Oops! Is that too radical for church?)"*
- *"People thinking you have to choose between the Lord and the environment"*
- *"Hardly anyone tithes"*
- *"When it tries to protect its members by creating an 'us/them' mentality with the world rather than seeing itself as a servant of the world."*
- *"Anti-homosexual hysteria"*
- *"There is way to much concentration on money in the modern church."*
- *"Too much money spent on fancy furnishings, technology, and the building."*
- *"When it does not welcome someone based on some external detail."*
- *"Push their beliefs down peoples throats."*
- *"The condoning or ignoring the things that are sinful and wrong just to keep money coming in the church."*
- *"Way to much politics involved in church."*
- *"The ministers teach to make people dependent on him to receive knowledge, understanding and encouragement and not directly from God himself by their own faith."*
- *"Some older people want to not change as the future changes"*
- *"The average church member is Biblically illiterate and doesn't care"*
- *"Pastors want utmost respect when they are no better that the average person on the street"*
- *"Ministers who use the pulpit to push their own agendas, rather than God's truth."*
- *"Church leaders (and followers) speak and act towards one another WORSE and with less tolerance than the world tends to treat each other."*

- *"Leadership in the church is about power and control and not about fitness for the job nor spiritual maturity."*
- *"Televangelists"*

Church Staff on Church Behaviors
- *"Focused on itself."*
- *"Focused on information rather than transformational living."*
- *"Pity the adulteress searching for the place that says 'we don't condemn you' but visits most churches."*
- *"Old folks checking out on serving just cause they're disgruntled with the music or change in general."*
- *"Superficial people"*
- *"Appears like a mindless, conservative self righteous group of un-accepting arrogant do-gooders."*
- *"Its a middle-class, money machine fixated on large staffs and big buildings not ministry to a lost and dying world."*
- *"The massive surplus of knowledge combined with the extreme lack of action from that knowledge."*
- *"The 90% of the time churches sit empty combined with all the money spent on building the vacant monstrosities."*
- *"Church marketing...apart from just living life and sharing the Gospel."*
- *"We're not smokin' what we're sellin' - not willing to FORGIVE each other...easier to move on to another place than deal w' the challenge at hand"*
- *"Expect people to come to them instead of going to where the people are"*
- *"Lack of authenticity in preachers, worship leaders, ushers, greeters, whoever."*
- *"Irrelevant in our communities."*
- *"That we are more of an institution than an organic body"*

Non-Christians on Church Behaviors

- *"Do not feel welcome"*
- *"The people don't do the things they tell me to do"*
- *"What happened to helping your fellow man? Who ever said that in order to help your neighbor, they had to follow your path to God."*
- *"They all preach love, but really practice hate."*
- *"My way or 'you're going to hell' attitude"*
- *"HOMOPHOBIA!!!!!!!!!!!!!!!! I know not all churches are homophobic but enough of them are. When are they going to learn that gays are people like us?"*
- *"Not allowed to think for myself"*
- *"The massive buildings! Are they a church or a business? I say business."*
- *"How seculars get blamed for everything. We're known as 'the world' and we love nothing but sex, drugs, food, anything hedonistic. Of course we're not the kind to raise children, go to work, do good deeds...."*

Beliefs of the Church

Christians / Church Staff on Church Beliefs

Contributions that could be allocated to this category by Christians or Church Staff were predictably few. Again, this likely results from those in our Christian and Church Staff categories not having a quarrel with the beliefs of a Church to which they belong. There were a couple of comments though.

- *"It is black or white--there are no gray areas."*
- *"Dogma"*

Non-Christians on Church Beliefs

This is a category where we would naturally expect some pushback from non-Christians. If they do not buy into the behaviors of the Church then they are likely not going to support the beliefs of the Church either. A summary of their comments is as follows.

- *"How almost every religion is 'the one true path'"*
- *"Tithing. It's like modern indulgences."*
- *"How sometimes it breeds hatred for things like diversity, science (social or otherwise), original thinking."*
- *"It promotes begging (praying), and so demeans humanity."*
- *"It promotes mental illness. You would have to be crazy to read the bible and take it seriously."*
- *"It leads people to devalue their own reason, and accept the most preposterous views of the universe and nature."*
- *"It tells people that they are sinners and creates guilt by mythology."*
- *"I find the brainwashing of children abhorrent. This is done in all churches, whether in places where people squat and memorize the Koran, or*

mindlessly claim to have a personal relationship with Jesus, or claim to 'channel' some other dead man or woman."
• "It promotes 'faith' over reason. It encourages people to accept hallucinations and gibberish, over scientific evidence."
• "It promotes poverty and ignorance, it tells people that it is better to 'believe' than know."

Miscellaneous Church Beliefs

And, of course, there are those comments that did not fit neatly into either category.

Christians on Church Behaviors - Miscellaneous

• "Not having to enough time to talk with the people I love most"
• "I am loosing my home, job & everything else because the church needs a new building (the old one isn't even full) and I am suppose to wait on the Lord!"
• "The 'CHURCHES' pick and choose who they help & how & if you show them Bible scripture they act like your not good enough to interpret scripture."
• "It shows favoritism on the basis of physical beauty."
• "It mistakes people skills for righteousness."

Church Staff on Church Behaviors - Miscellaneous

• "The little wafer you get during communion...why can't it be bigger? Not like a meal, just bigger. The same goes for the cup of wine/juice as well as the golf pencil they give you to fill out all the forms."
• "The 80/20 rule...80 percent of the work done by 20 percent of the people."

Non-Christians on Church Behaviors Misc.
- *"Waste of time"*
- *"The music"*

Love Church
And last but not least, there were those who were quite complimentary toward their church.

Christians on Loving Church
- *"Church is a great place. No other comments. You get a lift when you see people you know."*
- *"They are inviting and always willing to answer my questions."*
- *"I love to worship God"*
- *"I love to hang out with people who love God to"*
- *"You can make lifelong friends at church"*
- *"Church is fun"*
- *"Every week of my high school life I look forward to Sunday and Wednesday when I can worship god with my fellow Christians...soooo...I LOVE CHURCH!...anyone who says they don't like church and is a Christian is going to the wrong church...if your not a Christian then what do you know about church anyway? It is a different experience when you are saved."*

Conclusions

In an effort to better understand our test results, let's place all of our data into a single graphic and see what it reveals. The vertical axis indicates the percentage of contributions in a particular category and the horizontal axis identifies the 4 categories.

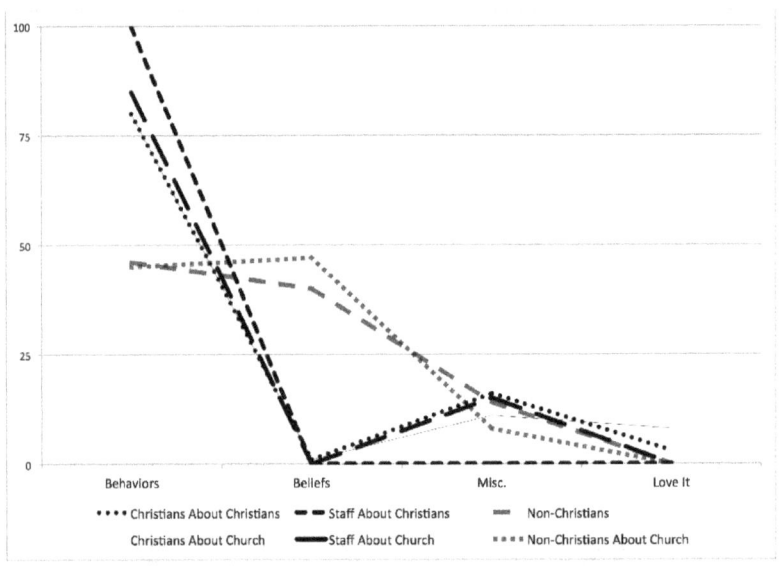

One does not have to be a rocket scientist (as cool as that would be) or a full time researcher (not quite as cool) to see our diagnostic testing has uncovered some pretty dramatic results.

1) Christians seem to strongly object to the behaviors of their fellow Christians *and* their Church while at the same time having no quarrel with the beliefs that one would hope inspires them both.

2) Non-Christians are close to being equally appalled by both the behaviors and beliefs of Christians and their Church.

Even though the test results seem to strongly suggest we (as Christians and the Church) have a problem behaving in ways that support the beliefs we claim to embrace, to fully understand our condition we need to ask some more questions.

1) How did we, as Christians, get to the point where our beliefs and our behaviors exist at such great distance from one another? (Historical) Chapter 4, 5, & 6

2) What rehabilitative strategies might we prescribe to aid in the realignment of our behaviors with our beliefs? (Treatment Plan) Chapter 7

3) What resistance might we encounter on this road to rehabilitation? (Is Your Big But the Problem?) Chapter 8

4) How do we move forward? Chapter 9

It is to these questions we now turn.

Part 3 - Literature Review

Chapter 4 – Creation Semiotics

Diagnostic Inquiry: Reviewing The Literature on the Topic.

Oftentimes when confronted with a difficult diagnosis, the diagnostician will consult the literature on the topic to be sure they understand potential contributing factors as well as better enable themselves to determine a proper treatment plan. In the world of medicine this might involve reviewing the medical journals for insights into the apparent condition or consulting the PDR (Physicians Desk Reference) for information on medications, potential side effects, and complications that can arise due to a particular course of action.

And so, in remaining true to our role as ecclesial diagnosticians, we too should pursue a course of due diligence in which we consult the literature on the topic in hopes of better understanding not only the condition of our Church, but of determining a path forward and out of its current dysfunctional state. Fortunately, we have a great resource for understanding these issues. It is a resource that has been around for thousands of years and continues to inspire Christians worldwide: the Bible.

Semiotics

When consulting the literature in an effort to better understand Christianity and our Church, it doesn't take long before we bump up against the idea of the kingdom. We briefly discussed the kingdom earlier when investigating the politics of Jesus for he was indeed a king of this invisible kingdom. But this idea of a kingdom did not arrive with Jesus in the New

Testament. In many ways, God's intention and solution has always been a kingdom solution. As such, the Bible can be understood as the story of the birthing of that kingdom.

One of the things we do not often see discussed when researching the kingdom is the shared imagery associated with the kingdom creation stories. To better understand these connections we need to heighten our semiotic awareness. Semiotic awareness? Yes, semiotic awareness. But, before we begin to semiotically explore these creation/kingdom connections, let's establish a baseline of understanding concerning the field of study known as *semiotics*.

Semiotics, in the most basic of explanations, is the study of signs; not just signs in the Bible, but signs that enable us to live in this world. A sign is something that stands for something else. These signs take the form of "words, images, sounds, gestures and objects."[94] In a very literal sense, "we live in a world of signs and we have no way of understanding anything except through signs and the codes into which they are organized."[95] This may seem like a bold or confusing statement but stick with me.

A sign is made up of two components: the *signifier* and the *signified*. No sign has any meaning apart from the meaning we have assigned to it. For example, let's take a look at words…this book is full of them.

Words are how we communicate with one another. In the English language, we have 26 letters from which we construct our words. Each letter is a symbol upon which we have a

---

[94] Daniel Chandler, *Semiotics: the Basics*, 2nd ed. (New York: Routledge, 2007), 2.
[95] Ibid., 11.

shared understanding of meaning. The letter A has no meaning apart from that which we have assigned it. We know it as the first letter of our alphabet, but we also know it to have additional meanings:

- It is the highest letter grade you can achieve on an academic test.

- It typically signifies good quality in products such as meat.

- It can stand alone in a sentence or it can be used with other symbols (letters) to construct other words.

The word for these words is…word… the letter *w* followed by the letter *o* followed by the letter *r* followed by the letter *d*. We have all come to agree that when you assemble these four letters in this particular order…*word*…you are talking about the images you are reading on this page, among other things.

Letters can also be grouped together in sequences that we do not recognize as *words* but still have meaning attached. For example, the sequence of letters QWERTY may just look like just a random collection of letters without any recognizable meaning. But, to those who are somewhat more tech savvy, QWERTY is associated with and identifies the layout of a standard computer keyboard: the top left letters on the standard computer keyboard contain the keys QWERTY.

For another example let's look at this letter sequence: WYSIWYG. Once again, this sequence can be seen as just a random series of letters without meaning, but to those familiar with this sequence, WYSIWYG is an acronym for What You See Is What You Get.

We use these sorts of letter sequences all the time. In a semiotic sense, the sequences QWERTY or WYSIWYG are signs that signify something else. In this sequence, QWERTY points to an object while WYSIWYG points to a concept or idea. They are signs in that they are composed of *signifier* and *signified*...as such...they have meaning.

Now let's talk a bit about these things we call *words* and their meaning. First let's look at the word *smoke*. The Oxford dictionary defines the word "smoke" as "a visible suspension of carbon or other particles in the air, typically one emitted from a burning substance." While this is a valid definition of the word "*smoke*", *smoke* can be a sign of different things. *Smoke* from a chimney is not cause for concern. *Smoke* coming from under the eaves of a house is cause for concern. Both of these examples are of *smoke*, and yet each would impact us quite differently. The meaning contained within the word *smoke*, as is the case with many words, is contextual. The meaning of the word *smoke* would be better understood by looking at what was signified by the *smoke*. "*Smoke*" can also be a verb: one *smokes* a cigarette. It can be a noun: "Hey, do you have some *smokes*?" It can also be an adjective: "That car is *smokin*." In this case the car is not on fire... no cause for concern. Of course if the sentence referred to smoke coming from under the hood of the car, in this context, there would indeed be cause for concern.

We string words together to make sentences. These sentences contain meaning, although their meaning is not always as obvious as it may seem on the surface. The following example illustrates how meaning is challenged by interpretation...with our understanding what is signified.

Suppose a grandfather says to his granddaughter the following: "I didn't eat Grandmother's chocolate cake." On the surface this sentence seems pretty self-explanatory, however this sentence can be interpreted in a variety of ways.⁹⁶

> "**I** didn't eat Grandmother's chocolate cake.
>
> (Paul ate Grandmother's chocolate cake.)
>
> I didn't **eat** Grandmother's chocolate cake.
>
> (I sat on Grandmother's chocolate cake.)
>
> I didn't eat **Grandmother's** chocolate cake.
>
> (I ate Susan's chocolate cake.)
>
> I didn't eat Grandmother's **chocolate** cake.
>
> (I ate Grandmother's fruitcake.)
>
> I didn't eat Grandmother's chocolate **cake**.
>
> (I ate Grandmother's chocolate cookie.)"

Our interpretation is variable and depends on a great many things.

To complicate the situation further, that which is signified by a sign can change over time. For example, the word "bad" used to have a pretty clear meaning. But now "bad" can be a good thing. The word "fly" used to mean an act similar to that of a bird. But, once again "fly" is now a complementary term. The word "text" used to refer to the words of a book or the actual book. Now millions are "texting" all over the world. Words are signs. What is signified by these signs is contextual and cultural; to fully grasp what is being communicated we need to factor both of these into our understanding.

---

⁹⁶ Sean Hall, *This Means This, This Means That: A User's Guide to Semiotics* (London: Laurence King Publishers, 2007), 30.

The meaning of words can also change while retaining their emotional impact. For example, the dictionary defines the word "fire" as "combustion or burning, in which substances combine chemically with oxygen from the air and typically give out bright light, heat and smoke."[97] Again, this is technically correct, but it reflects a more modern understanding of fire removed from its historical meaning. Initially, fire was likely a life or death word…with fire there was survival…without fire, survival was more difficult. Fire would have brought about an emotional response. Fire was a cooked meal. Fire was comfort on a cold night. Fire was a defense against the wild ones lurking in the woods. Today, fire is available to most of us, at least in the Western world, with the flick of a switch. Fire is common and commonplace. As such, fire has lost its emotional connection in much of the world. Unless of course one is "fired" from their place of employment, in which case much of the original emotion is re-attached. When one is fired, survival is more difficult, cooked meals may become scarce, the nights could become cold and one's defense against the creditors lurking in the woods would be diminished. It is easy to see how the term *fired* likely came to be associated with the emotion and security of a fire.

Social media is rich with signs that add to our ability to communicate because, as we have seen, *text* outside of *context* can convey a variety of meanings. Have you ever sent a text or an email to someone and had the recipient take it completely wrong? I think we all have. What you intended to be a tongue in cheek comment ended up offending them because they

---

[97] Oxford Dictionary,
http://www.oxforddictionaries.com/us/definition/american_english/fire?q=fire

misread the intention of your message? But, in an effort to insure our textual conversations are received in the manner in which they are sent, we now have something at our disposal we like to call *emoticons*. Emoticons are those little symbols that add emotion to the text: :), :(, :0, :}, :P. We also have other little acronyms such as: lol, rofl, imho etc. The point of each of these is to add clarity to our message or perhaps act as shorthand in our efforts to communicate, and as such, they are signs.

There is one more concept we need to cover on this topic before we move on. It is the idea of semiotic awareness. For an example, take the stop sign. No, don't take the stop sign; just take it as an example. (See, when using words we have to be specific about the meaning we intend.) A stop sign is very appropriately called a sign. It is a red octagon with the word STOP on it. We all know when you see this sign, your car is supposed to cease forward motion at the sign before progressing toward your destination. To some people in my neighborhood a STOP sign apparently has a slightly different meaning in that they just slow down or maybe not even that. But, enough about me…

Now let's talk about the color of the stop sign…red. In many instances the color red signifies some degree of danger…red fire trucks, red ambulances, and red lights. In the context of an intersection, a red light means the same thing a stop sign means. In the case of a traffic light, we have red for stop, yellow for caution, and green for go. You know what these colors mean and respond accordingly. You exist in a state of semiotic awareness in that your senses are trained to recognize these signs for what they mean and therefore you are able to respond appropriately.

Perhaps one of the best examples of having a heightened semiotic awareness is revealed in something we can call the *new car experience*. Do you remember the time when you were either looking at a particular new car or had actually purchased a new car? And, do you remember how prior to your beginning to look at this particular model you can't remember seeing that many of them, but now you see them everywhere? This occurs because your senses are now sensitized to notice that particular automobile over and above those other vehicles on the road. It also carries with it the unfortunate consequence in that we do not feel as special as we thought we were.

And so, whether we knew it or not we have been and are semioticians whose awareness to certain things can vary depending on the degree to which we are paying attention. Now that we know a little bit about semiotics and as such have a heightened awareness to words and themes, let's revisit some Bible stories and look at them from our new semiotic perspective.

Creation Semiotics

Let's begin our semiotic journey to better understand the kingdom of God by looking at three creation stories in the Bible. The first we will call *original creation* as told in the first two chapters of Genesis, the second we will call *re-creation* which is the story of Noah and the flood found in Genesis 8, and the third we will call *new creation* which is the story of Jesus found in the New Testament.

For our investigation we will use the following texts. I have highlighted some of the key words in bold text to heighten our semiotic awareness a bit.

Original Creation

*"In the beginning when God created the **heavens** and the earth, the earth was a formless void and darkness covered the face of the deep, while a **wind** from God swept over the face of the **waters**."*[98]

*"And God said, 'Let the **waters** under the sky be gathered together into one place, and let the dry land appear.' And it was so. God called the dry land Earth, and the **waters** that were gathered together he called Seas. And God saw that **it was good**."*[99]

Here is a graphic that can help heighten our semiotic awareness to four elements of the original creation story we want to discuss:

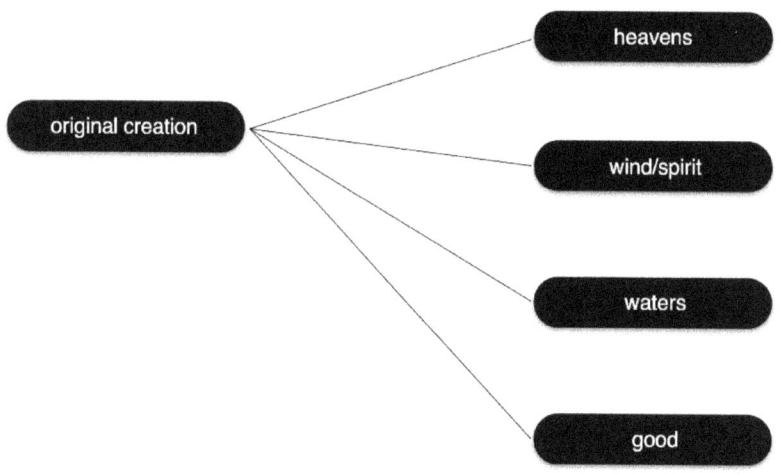

---

[98] Genesis 1:1-2. (emphasis added)
[99] Genesis 1:9-10. (emphasis added)

Re-Creation

"But God remembered Noah and all the wild animals and all the domestic animals that were with him in the ark. And God made a **wind** blow over the earth, and the **waters** subsided; the fountains of the deep and the windows of the **heavens** were closed, the rain from the **heavens** was restrained, and the **waters** gradually receded from the earth." [100]

"At the end of forty days Noah opened the window of the ark that he had made and sent out the raven; and it went to and fro until the **waters** were dried up from the earth. Then he sent out the **dove** from him, to see if the **waters** had subsided from the face of the ground; but the **dove** found no place to set its foot, and it returned to him to the ark, for the **waters** were still on the face of the whole earth. So he put out his hand and took it and brought it into the ark with him. He waited another seven days, and again he sent out the **dove** from the ark; and the dove came back to him in the evening, and there in its beak was a freshly plucked olive leaf; so Noah knew that the **waters** had subsided from the earth. Then he waited another seven days, and sent out the **dove**; and it did not return to him any more." [101]

"And when the Lord **smelled the pleasing odor**, the Lord said in his heart, 'I will never again curse the ground because of humankind, for the inclination of the human heart is evil from youth; nor will I ever again destroy every living creature as I have done.'" [102]

---

[100] Genesis 8:1-3. (emphasis added)
[101] Genesis 8:6-12. (emphasis added)
[102] Genesis 8:21. (emphasis added)

This telling of the re-creation story adds a fifth element to our list of words: a dove.

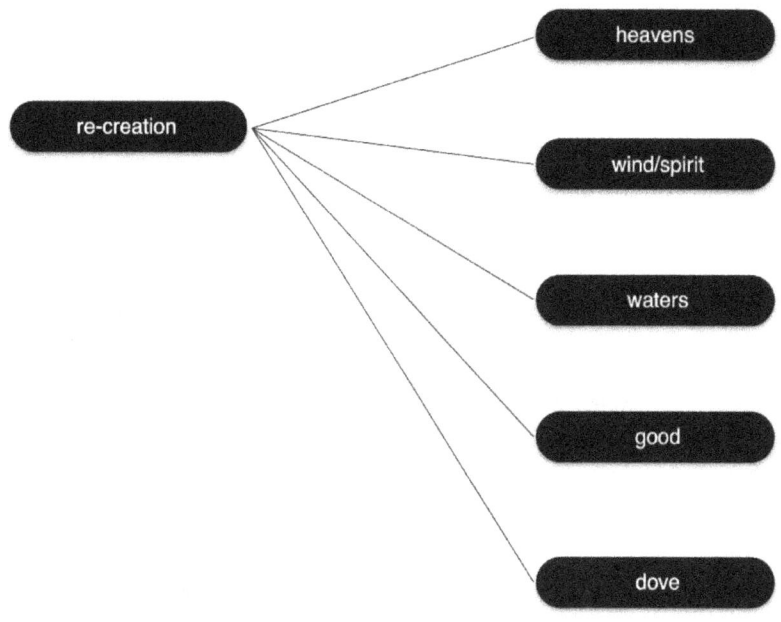

New Creation

*"And when Jesus had been baptized, just as he came up from the **water**, suddenly the **heavens** were opened to him and he saw the **Spirit** of God descending like a **dove** and alighting on him. And a voice from heaven said, 'This is my Son, the Beloved, with whom I am **well pleased.**'"*[103]

And now this graphic helps us see the same 5 elements in the new creation story:

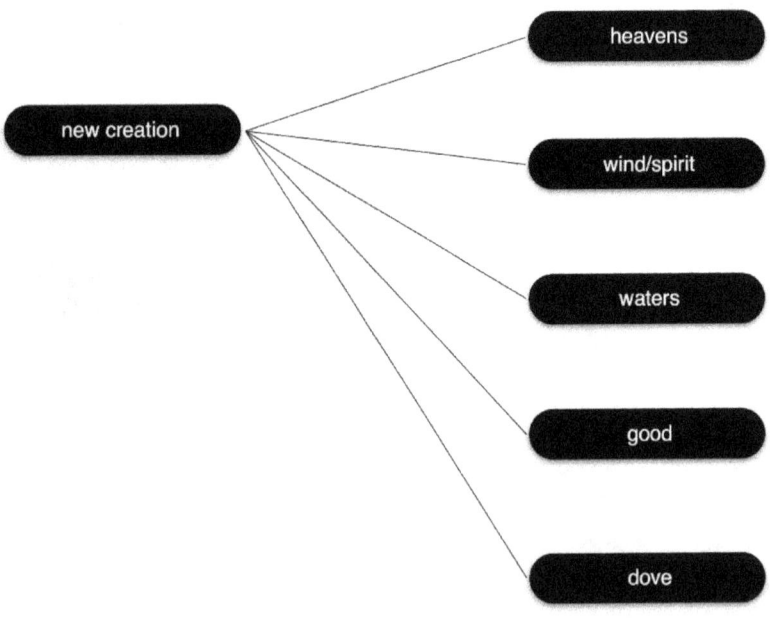

Likely your semiotic awareness is now heightened to the interesting way in which these words are repeated in these

---

[103] Matthew 3:16-17, Mark, 1:11, Luke 3:22. (emphasis added)

creation stories, but just to be sure we are all on the same page, here is a graphic in which these common elements are stacked upon one another for greater clarity:

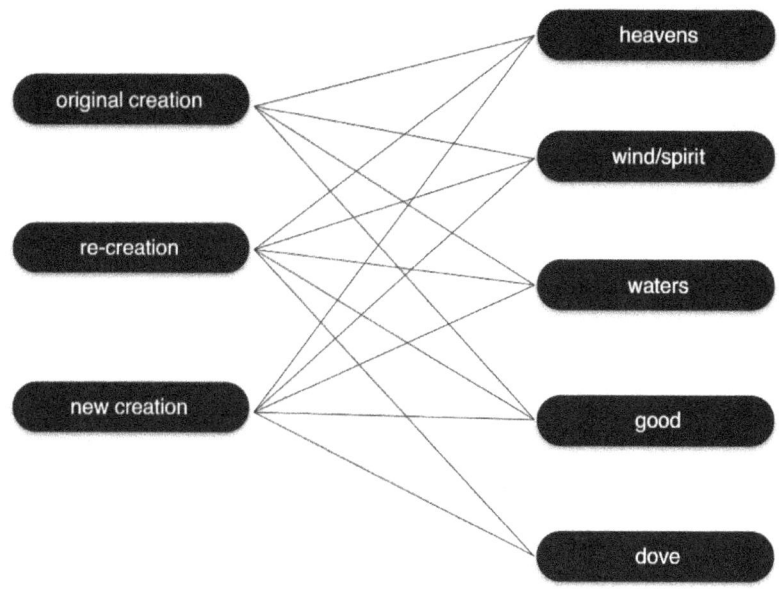

The writers of these stories did not use these particular words by accident. In the language of semiotics, these common elements were signs that have particular significance. Their use reveals a connective subtext or understory to the story we might miss if we did not pause to look a little deeper at what was being communicated.

Heavens - Heaven is sometimes connected to the space that surrounds our earth. However, heaven is oftentimes associated with the "abode of God."[104] We see God's throne in heaven,[105] God's sanctuary in heaven,[106] and God referred to

---

[104] Bromiley, *The International Standard Bible Encyclopedia: Vol. 2*, 654.

as "the God of heaven."[107] The mention of heaven in these stories identifies them as both extraordinary (not of this world) and connected to God.

Wind - While the NRSV translates the Hebrew word *ruach* as wind in Genesis 1:2, other translations such as NLT, KJV and NIV translate it as "spirit." In fact, it can be translated as breath, air, wind, or spirit.[108] And so it was a wind...a spirit wind...the very breath of God that hovered over the waters in creation, just as it was a spirit wind that blew over the floodwaters in the story of Noah causing them to subside.

Water - In the original creation, water covered the earth, but these waters were gathered together allowing the solid ground to be revealed making life.[109]

In the re-creation, the waters flooded the earth, extinguishing all of humanity apart from Noah and the survivors in the ark, but once again dry land emerged from the waters enabling humanity to inhabit God's creation.[110]

In the new creation we see a revisiting of this theme, as the first born of the new creation...Jesus...rises up out of the water of John's baptism.

Good - At the end of each of these 3 creation events, God makes the same proclamation: it is "good." We see this in the original creation story as God pronounces the goodness of creation seven times.[111] In the re-creation story God does not

---

[105] Psalm 14:2, 103.19, etc.
[106] Psalm 102:19, Hebrews 19:24.
[107] Gen 24:3, 2 Chronicles 36:23, etc.
[108] Young, *Young's Analytical Concordance to the Bible*, 114.
[109] Genesis 1:9.
[110] Genesis 8:11.

come right out and say the words "it is good." However, we can see an indication that God determined the re-creation to be good through God declaring it had a "pleasing odor"[112] in conjunction with God's promise to never destroy the earth again[113]...a good thing. And, in the new creation story God announces the goodness of Jesus...the first born of the new creation: *"This is my Son, the Beloved, with whom I am* **well pleased**.*"*[114]

Dove - In the original creation story, we do not have direct reference to a dove, even though several translations refer to God's spirit as "hovering over the waters;"[115] a somewhat bird like reference. The Message goes further in this direction by saying "God's Spirit brooded like a bird above the watery abyss."[116] In any event, we do see the image of a dove used directly in the re-creation story of Noah to announce re-creation is ready for its inhabitants...the visible confirmation of God's intention to enable new life. We also see a dove at the baptism of Jesus used as a way to describe God's spirit descending upon Jesus and as such it is a dove once again that indicates the dawning of a new creation life.

---

[111] Genesis 1:4,10,12,18, 21, 25, 31.
[112] Genesis 8:21.
[113] Genesis 8:22.
[114] Matthew 3:16-17, Mark, 1:11, Luke 3:22.
[115] Genesis 1:2 NIV
[116] Genesis 1:2 MSG

Semiotic Summary

Our semiotic exploration of these creation stories has revealed connective tissue between these stories we might otherwise have missed. The common elements of *heaven, wind/spirit, water, good* and *dove* in these stories are all signs; signs that are there to make sure the reader or hearer of these stories doesn't miss their significance and connection. In each of them God is doing what God does: creating, re-creating, and ultimately, through Jesus, birthing a new creation into existence…a new kingdom.

Chapter 5 – Understanding the Kingdom

Just to make sure we're not heading down some kind of *new kingdom* rabbit hole in our diagnostic investigation, let's first ascertain the significance of the kingdom in Jesus' message. As we begin this exploration, one of the first things we uncover is the New Testament records Jesus mentioning the kingdom approximately 150[117] times. In fact, it can be said, "one of the few things biblical scholars agree on is that the kingdom of God was the cornerstone of Jesus' preaching."[118] If this is the case, let's see what we can learn about this *new kingdom* Jesus spent so much time talking about.

Expectation of a Kingdom

As Jesus began to live out his role in history, he did so in the midst of an oppressed people who lived with the expectation of a coming Messiah; a rescuer to deliver them from their troubles. However, this anticipation manifest in dueling Messianic visions as there were two competing schools of thought concerning the role of this coming Messiah.

From one perspective, "the Messiah was to inherit all the promises given to David, Israel's first anointed king, and like David was to be a political ruler."[119] While at the same time, rabbinic literature envisioned "the coming of the eschatological future as a creative act of God by which this world is remade

---

[117] Young, *Young's Analytical Concordance to the Bible*, 573-574.
[118] Leonard I. Sweet, *Giving Blood: A Fresh Paradigm for Preaching* (Grand Rapids, MI: Zondervan, 2014), 71.
[119] Bromiley, *The International Standard Bible Encyclopedia: Vol. 3*, 332.

rather than as a mere restoration or reform of the nation's political or social life."[120] In spite of these somewhat contradictory views, both camps "firmly believed that the day would come when God would intervene in order to restore Israel and fulfill the promise of a Kingdom of peace and justice."[121]

In Luke, we see Jesus closely associated with the expectation of a new kingdom.

> *"As they were listening to this, he went on to tell a parable, because he was near Jerusalem, and because they supposed that the kingdom of God was to appear immediately."*[122]

And, in Jesus' triumphal entry into Jerusalem, we see the people connecting Jesus with the more political leaning Messianic expectation through a connection with David.

> *"Hosanna to the Son of David! Blessed is the one who comes in the name of the Lord! Hosanna in the highest heaven!"*[123]

Interestingly, this praiseful accolade references Psalm 118; the reflections of an oppressed people whose trust in God has been rewarded with the arrival of their rescuer. To better understand the depth of meaning in this psalm, lets take a look at a few excerpts.

> *"Out of my distress I called on the Lord; the Lord answered me and set me in a broad place. With the Lord on my side I do not fear. What can mortals do to me? The Lord is on my side to help me; I shall look in triumph on those who hate me."*[124]

---

[120] Ibid..
[121] Gonzales, *The Story of Christianity*, 11.
[122] Luke 19:11.
[123] Matthew 21:9, Mark 11:9-10. John 12:13.

"I was pushed hard, so that I was falling, but the Lord helped me. The Lord is my strength and my might; he has become my salvation."[125]

"This is the gate of the Lord; the righteous shall enter through it. I thank you that you have answered me and have become my salvation."[126]

"Save us, we beseech you, O Lord! O Lord, we beseech you, give us success! Blessed is the one who comes in the name of the Lord. We bless you from the house of the Lord. The Lord is God, and he has given us light. Bind the festal procession with branches, up to the horns of the altar. You are my God, and I will give thanks to you; you are my God, I will extol you. O give thanks to the Lord, for he is good, for his steadfast love endures forever."[127]

It is also interesting to note as Jesus entered Jerusalem on the back of a donkey the crowds shouted *hosanna*[128] which means, *"Save, we pray thee!"*[129] echoing the first words of Psalm 118:25. When we begin to understand these connections and what they are signifying, it becomes clear the people of the day felt their Messianic expectation was being fulfilled in Jesus.

---

[124] Psalm 118 5-7.
[125] Psalm 118:13-14.
[126] Psalm 118:20-21.
[127] Psalm 118:25-29.
[128] Matthew 21:9, Mark 11:9-10. John 12:13.
[129] Young, *Young's Analytical Concordance to the Bible*, 492.

Evidence of the Kingdom

When we look for evidence of the arrival of the Messiah and his kingdom we find ourselves in the company of John...one whose mission was to announce and prepare the world for the coming of this new king and his kingdom.

When John heard the stories of the miraculous events surrounding Jesus, he sent some of his followers to ask Jesus if He was the one...the Messiah they had been waiting for.

> *"John the Baptist has sent us to you to ask, 'Are you the one who is to come, or are we to wait for another?' Jesus had just then cured many people of diseases, plagues, and evil spirits, and had given sight to many who were blind. And he answered them, 'Go and tell John what you have seen and heard: the blind receive their sight, the lame walk, the lepers are cleansed, the deaf hear, the dead are raised, the poor have good news brought to them. And blessed is anyone who takes no offense at me.'"*[130]

It is interesting to our discussion to note the confirmation of the Messiah's arrival was not based upon whether Jesus had the proper beliefs or the proper schooling or whether he came from the more appropriate side of the tracks; Messianic fulfillment was based upon Jesus' actions: the deaf could hear again, the dead were being raised back to life, and those who culture had relegated to the sidelines of life were being embraced and invited into fellowship. These were *signs* that *signified* (remember our semiotics discussion) the arrival of the Messiah and his kingdom. As such, it was what Jesus did that verified the truth of his identity. In Jesus, the kingdom had truly come as

---

[130] Luke 7:20-23

expressed in the prayer Jesus taught the disciples...*on earth as it is in heaven.*[131]

Longing for a Kingdom

Not only was there an expectation of the kingdom's arrival, there also appears to have been a kind of longing for this new kingdom. To find evidence of this, we need look no further than the prayer Jesus taught His disciples to pray:

> *"Our Father which art in heaven, Hallowed be thy name. Thy kingdom come. Thy will be done in earth, as it is in heaven. Give us this day our daily bread. And forgive us our debts, as we forgive our debtors. And lead us not into temptation, but deliver us from evil: For thine is the kingdom, and the power, and the glory, forever. Amen."*[132]

Some might say the kingdom reference in the prayer refers to that day in that future in which Jesus returns and God's kingdom is fully manifest, but to better understand, let us consider the context in which it was delivered. The disciples were receiving instructions on how and what to pray for their daily existence (not for some future date) as we see evidenced by the requests to *give us our daily bread, forgive us as we forgive others, and help us avoid temptation.* This is a prayer for the here and now and not a prayer for some future eschatological moment. And so, in these examples we see not only an expectation of a coming kingdom, but a prayerful longing for the presence of that kingdom in the here and now.

---

[131] Matthew 6:10.
[132] Matthew 6:9-13.

Proclamation of the Kingdom

This news of this kingdom was not private knowledge for a privileged few; it was announced and proclaimed for all who would listen: *"The law and the prophets were in effect until John came; since then the good news of the kingdom of God is proclaimed."*[133]

In Luke 8 we have another instance in which we are told Jesus traveled the countryside *"proclaiming and bringing the good news of the kingdom of God."*[134] And in another story, after a day of healing, Jesus got away by himself but was pursued by the crowd who tried to convince Him not to leave, *"But he said to them, 'I must proclaim the good news of the kingdom of God to the other cities also; for I was sent for this purpose.'"*[135]

Good news...the kingdom of God...the reason Jesus was sent: all of these combine to help us understand the primacy of the kingdom of God in and through Jesus.

Arrival of the Kingdom

So, if the kingdom was being announced and proclaimed, what do we know about its arrival? We know that after a time of testing in the desert, Jesus proclaimed: *"Repent, for the kingdom of heaven has come near."*[136] In this, we have the language *"has come"* indicative of something that has happened. But we also the addition of the word *"near."*[137] Therefore, we can take this

---

[133] Luke 16:16.
[134] Luke 8:1.
[135] Luke 4:43-44, Mark 1:38.
[136] Matthew 4:17, Mark 1:14.

statement to mean the kingdom is *coming* and is in fact *close*, but not yet fully "consummated."[138] In other words, it is an already, but not yet kingdom.

The Already/Not Yet Kingdom

As is true with many things concerning God, we find the kingdom of God existing in somewhat of a paradox. To better understand this paradox, let's look to the way in which Jesus refers to this paradoxical kingdom. First of all, Jesus has a tendency to refer to the kingdom in very earthy here and now terms. We have the kingdom being referred to as a *good seed* (Matthew 13:24, Mark 4:26), *a mustard seed* (Matthew 13:31, Mark 4:31, Luke 13:19) as well as *yeast* (Matthew 13:33, Luke 13:21). These are very tangible and present metaphors that link the understanding of the kingdom to the here and now. However, these items Jesus referred to are not static things. Each one of them is something that exists in one state, but then transitions or grows into something else. It is not as if Jesus said the kingdom of God is like a boat that allows you to take a trip to a new place, or like a net that allows you to catch more fish. No, the kingdom is like something that both *is* and *is yet to come*: something that is not *stationary* but also has *potentiality* embedded within it.

Jesus does not spend a great deal of time talking about a future kingdom. Instead, he seems much more concerned with birthing this eternal kingdom in the here and now. However,

---

[137] Matthew 4:17, Mark 1:14.
[138] James A. Brooks, "The Kingdom of God in The New Testament." *Southwestern Journal Of Theology* 40, no. 2 (March 1, 1998): 36.

this is not to say Jesus never references some kind of future kingdom. One example of this occurs as Jesus was on his way to Jerusalem.

> "A bystander said, 'Master, will only a few be saved?' 'Whether few or many is none of your business. Put your mind on your life with God. The way to life - to God! - is vigorous and requires your total attention.'"[139]

Here we see Jesus dismissing the question concerning the future as he attempts to underscore the importance of the kingdom life in the here and now. However, he does go on to address the question.

> "A lot of you are going to assume that you'll sit down to God's salvation banquet just because you've been hanging around the neighborhood all your lives. Well, one day you're going to be banging on the door, wanting to get in, but you'll find the door locked and the Master saying, 'Sorry, you're not on my guest list.' You'll protest, 'But we've known you all our lives!' only to be interrupted with his abrupt, 'Your kind of knowing can hardly be called knowing. You don't know the first thing about me.'"[140]

While this does refer to a future eschatological event, it is fairly apparent that this event is contingent upon the here and now as if to further underscore the importance of living a kingdom life in the present.

If we are willing to accept the kingdom as primary to Jesus' message, the question arises; did this message continue in the Church post-resurrection? Fortunately, we have many

---

[139] Luke 13:23-24. (MSG)
[140] Luke 13:24-27. (MSG)

examples in the writings of Paul to support the position that the kingdom of God remained a primary concern to at least this early leader of the church. Here is a selection of scriptures from Paul's ongoing story of the Church found in the book of Acts as a way to underscore the importance of the kingdom in the writings of Paul.

> • *"But when they believed Philip, who was proclaiming the good news about the kingdom of God and the name of Jesus Christ, they were baptized, both men and women."*[141]
>
> • *"There they strengthened the souls of the disciples and encouraged them to continue in the faith, saying, 'It is through many persecutions that we must enter the kingdom of God.'"*[142]
>
> •*"He entered the synagogue and for three months spoke out boldly, and argued persuasively about the kingdom of God."*[143]
>
> • *"After they had set a day to meet with him, they came to him at his lodgings in great numbers. From morning until evening he explained the matter to them, testifying to the kingdom of God and trying to convince them about Jesus both from the Law of Moses and from the prophets."*[144]
>
> • *"For the kingdom of God is not food and drink but righteousness and peace and joy in the Holy Spirit."*[145]
>
> • *"Then comes the end, when he hands over the kingdom to God the Father, after he has destroyed every ruler and every authority and power."*[146]

---

[141] Acts 9:12.
[142] Acts 14:2.
[143] Acts 19:8.
[144] Acts 28:23.
[145] Romans 15:7.

> • *"He has rescued us from the power of darkness and transferred us into the kingdom of his beloved Son."*[147]
>
> • *"In the presence of God and of Christ Jesus, who is to judge the living and the dead, and in view of his appearing and his kingdom, I solemnly urge you: proclaim the message; be persistent whether the time is favorable or unfavorable; convince, rebuke, and encourage, with the utmost patience in teaching."*[148]
>
> • *"Therefore, since we are receiving a kingdom that cannot be shaken, let us give thanks, by which we offer to God an acceptable worship with reverence and awe; for indeed our God is a consuming fire."*[149]

While it is not my preference to simply cite verse after verse, hearing the writer in his own words express both the here and now as well as the future aspects of the kingdom underscores it's importance in the writings of Paul.

Entrance Into the Kingdom

So, if there is this already/not yet kingdom, what do we know about our ability to enter into it?

• We know we must be born into the kingdom - born of both flesh and spirit:

> *"'Very truly, I tell you, no one can see the kingdom of God without being born from above.' Nicodemus said to him, 'How can anyone be born after having grown old? Can one enter a second time into*

---

[146] 1 Corinthians 15:24.
[147] Colossians 1:13.
[148] 2 Timothy 4:1-2.
[149] Hebrews 12:28-29.

the mother's womb and be born?' Jesus answered, 'Very truly, I tell you, no one can enter the kingdom of God without being born of water and Spirit'"[150]

- We know we must receive the kingdom in a child-like manner:

"Truly I tell you, whoever does not receive the kingdom of God as a little child will never enter it."[151]

- We know wealth presents certain challenges:

"Then Jesus looked around and said to his disciples, 'How hard it will be for those who have wealth to enter the kingdom of God!'"[152]

- And then there is this worrisome warning:

"Not everyone who says to me, 'Lord, Lord,' will enter the kingdom of heaven, but only the one who does the will of my Father in heaven."[153]

To review, we have uncovered the following concerning the kingdom:

- There was an expectation of a coming kingdom.

- Jesus was evidence of the kingdom's arrival.

- There was a longing for the coming of the kingdom.

- The kingdom was proclaimed by Jesus.

- The kingdom is a now and not yet kingdom.

---

[150] John 3:5-8.
[151] Mark 10:15, Matthew 19:14, Luke 18:16.
[152] Mark 10:23, Matthew 19:23, Luke 18:24.
[153] Matthew 7:21.

- Those who followed Jesus also proclaimed the kingdom.
- We know the requirements for entry into the kingdom.

As our investigation revealed the importance of the kingdom and the role it should play in our lives as followers of Jesus, several questions arise:

- How should the kingdom manifest in our life?
- How should the kingdom manifest in our churches?
- Do we see any evidence of kingdom living in either of these locales?

As a way to help answer these questions, let's look to Jesus for clues as to what a kingdom life or kingdom living might look like.

Chapter 6 - The Identity of Jesus

In our earlier discussion of semiotics, we learned whenever we see something repeated in a variety of contexts, we should pay special attention so we don't miss the significance of the reference. This repetition would be similar (although not exactly the same) as tossing a song lyric or a movie reference into a conversation so that those who know the reference will make the connection and understand the implications of what is being said.

For example, years ago... a movie came out called *Caddyshack* starring Bill Murray as the character Bill Murray plays so well. In one scene Bill is explaining to a young caddy an encounter he had with the Dalai Lama while caddying for him on the golf course. As the scene goes, at the end of the game, the Dalai Lama was apparently going to stiff Bill by not tipping him, but when pressured by Murray on the issue, the Dalai Lama told Bill, "When you die, on your death bed, you will receive total consciousness." Bill then very smugly announces to his friend... "So I got that going for me...which is nice." All this to say, in my life, whenever I want to connect some benefit I have received to the delusional confidence Mr. Murray places in his promise of total consciousness...placing my presumed benefit in its proper perspective, I say... "So I got that going for me...which is nice." And so, those who know me and are familiar with the reference understand my tongue-in-cheek explanation associated with some empty benefit.

In a somewhat less specific and personal reference, we see the same sort of inferences being made when people of a certain age group hear someone say "let it be." For these people it is natural to make a connection to the Beatles song with the same name. For different generations, perhaps "just beat it"[154] or "she came in like a wrecking ball"[155] would be better examples. These references are inserted into the conversation as a way to increase understanding or perhaps make a connection or a point. Therefore, lest we miss the point, let's engage in a bit of semiotic exploration concerning the identity of Jesus.

Trinitarian Realization

Even though the word *trinity* or a complete doctrine concerning the *trinity* is nowhere to be found in the scriptures, the *trinity* exists as a well-accepted concept within Christianity: it is a way to express and understand the three-in-one identity of our triune God: Father, Son, & Holy Spirit.

Interestingly, when Jesus made a statement concerning his identity to the disciples, he described himself in a rather triune manner: *"I am the way, and the truth, and the life"*[156]...three aspects of his identity manifest in the oneness of his presence.

While it is premature at this point in the Gospel narrative to expect those present to connect this in any way, shape, or form to the concept of the Trinity, this triune identity statement does echo a theme or motif found in quite a number of stories the hearers would likely have been familiar with from the Hebrew Bible.

---

[154] Michael Jackson - Beat It
[155] Miley Cyrus - Wrecking Ball
[156] John 14:6.

Here are a few examples:

- The Ark of the Covenant contained three items: a gold urn containing manna, Aaron's rod, and the tablets of the covenant.[157]

- Shadrach, Meshach, and Abednego (three individuals) triumphed over Nebuchadnezzar through the direct intervention of God.[158]

- Moses and Aaron petitioned Pharaoh for permission to travel three days into the desert to sacrifice to their God.[159]

- When Joshua was about to lead God's people into the promised land he told them: *"Prepare your provisions; for in three days you are to cross over the Jordan, to go in to take possession of the land that the Lord your God gives you to possess."*[160]

- Jonah found himself in the belly of the whale for three days.[161]

As semioticians, we know signs have significance. So what significance or connective tissue exists between these stories of *threes*? Well, on the most basic of levels, these triplets can be seen as a way to connect an individual story to the greater narrative of God…to God's miraculous presence and purpose in those stories.

From our vantage point years later, we can make Trinitarian connections to Jesus' triune identity, which might have been missed at the time. This does not mean however, the

---

[157] Hebrews 9:4.
[158] Daniel 3.
[159] Exodus 5:3.
[160] Joshua 1:11.
[161] Jonah 1:17.

divine implications of Jesus statement were lost on those present for when Jesus made the statement *"I am the way, and the truth, and the life,"*[162] this moved his announcement beyond the realm of insinuation as it directly connected Jesus with God's identity as revealed to Moses.

Moses, if you will remember, was rather reluctant to accept God's call to lead Israel out of captivity and in the process of coming to grips with what was being asked of him, he asked God a question:

> *"If I come to the Israelites and say to them, 'The God of your ancestors has sent me to you,' and they ask me, 'What is his name?' what shall I say to them?"*[163]

God responded.

> *"'I am who I am.' He said further, 'Thus you shall say to the Israelites, I am has sent me to you.'"*[164]

And so, Jesus' statement makes clear the Godly connection and significance of Jesus' proclamation: *"I am the way, and the truth, and the life."*[165]

Interestingly, this use of triplets to suggest the presence of God in the story is not confined to the Hebrew Bible for we find examples of this in the New Testament as well:

- Satan's temptation of Jesus[166] - three times.

- Peter's denial of Jesus[167] - three times.

---

[162] John 14:6.
[163] Exodus 3:13.
[164] Exodus 3:14.
[165] John 14:6.
[166] Matthew 4:1-11, Luke 4:1-13.

- Jesus' forgiveness of Peter [168] - three times.

- Jesus praying in Gethsemane[169] - three times.

- Days between crucifixion and resurrection - three days.[170]

- Jesus appeared to the disciples post resurrection – three times.[171]

While it is likely academics and theologians will have varying interpretations of the significance or lack thereof concerning this repetition,[172] we must at bare minimum acknowledge *threes* are associated with a variety of prominent stories in the history of our faith.

So, as a way to perhaps underscore and reveal the importance of his multi-faceted triune identity, Jesus announces himself as the *way*, the *truth* and the *life*; not just the *way* as an example of proper living; not just a philosophical *truth* to be pursued or debated; and not just an example of a *life* well lived...three aspects of a single one. As such, Jesus is a living example for all of us in how to live out our lives as Christians for the *way* of Jesus points to and makes visible the *truth* that enables a kingdom *life*.

---

[167] Matthew 26:69-75, Mark 14:66-72, Luke 22:56-62, John 18:17-27.
[168] John 21:15-17.
[169] Matthew 26:36-44, Mark 14:32-41.
[170] Matthew 12:40.
[171] Matthew 13:14
[172] For a good overview of "threes" in the Bible you can consult the following web article. https://bible.org/series/third-day-motif

Mission Statement

Mission statements are a way to clarify purpose. From an organizational standpoint, mission statements enable those both inside and outside the organization to understand the purpose of the institution. They hopefully help keep the organization focused on its original intent rather than venturing off into activities that deviate from that stated purpose.

From an individual point of view, a mission statement helps clarify those things that not only inspire but drive our actions and pursuits. Once again, without a clear understanding and commitment to a set of goals and preferred destinations, it is easy for us to wander in a variety of directions that ultimately lead to our going nowhere at all. Or, in the words of the great philosopher Yogi Berra: if you don't know where you are going, you might wind up someplace else.

The scriptures record several instances of Jesus announcing something we might identify as a personal mission statement: *"I came that they may have life, and have it abundantly"*[173] and *"I must proclaim the good news of the kingdom of God to the other cities also; for I was sent for this purpose."*[174]

As we saw earlier, Jesus was clear on His identity: *"I am the way, the truth, and the life."*[175]

---

[173] John 10:10. "I came so they can have real and eternal life, more and better life than they ever dreamed of ." MSG
[174] Luke 4:43-44, Mark 1:38.
[175] John 14:6.

And, now we can see he was clear on his purpose: proclaim of the good news of the kingdom[176] and enable an abundant life.[177]

This clarity of identity and purpose raises a question: was Jesus equally clear with His disciples on their purpose? Fortunately, for those of us whose purpose includes following Jesus, the scriptures shine a little light on this area as well.

Mission Statement for Discipleship

As Jesus was sending the disciples out on their first missionary journey, he informed them of their purpose:

"As you go, proclaim the good news, 'The kingdom of heaven has come near'. Cure the sick, raise the dead, cleanse the lepers, cast out demons."[178]

The disciples were to proclaim the good news of the kingdom *and* bring restoration to those in need. It is a mission statement that aligns with Jesus' purpose. Therefore in this instruction we have Jesus telling the disciples, in essence, to be reflections of him...those whose actions reveal the one who sent them...in other words... be Christ-like.

In another example, as Jesus was about to ascend into heaven, he left the disciples with a final word...a loving farewell...perhaps a reminder of that which he thought most important for them to remember. We know this parting thought as the Great Commission:

---

[176] Luke 4:43-44, Mark 1:38.
[177] Luke 4:43-44, Mark 1:38.
[178] Matthew 10:1-8, Mark 6:7-13, Luke 9:1-2.

"And Jesus came and said to them, 'All authority in heaven and on earth has been given to me. Go therefore and make disciples of all nations, baptizing them in the name of the Father and of the Son and of the Holy Spirit, and teaching them to obey everything that I have commanded you. And remember, I am with you always, to the end of the age.'"[179]

Oftentimes the primary message taken from this passage is that we should be missionaries to the world: teaching, preaching, baptizing, and spreading the good news…a beliefs based purpose. While this is technically correct, it leaves out an important part of the story for Jesus also told them to teach these new disciples to obey everything He commanded. Obey? Wait…what are we supposed to obey? What did Jesus command us to do?

"This is my commandment, that you love one another as I have loved you. No one has greater love than this, to lay down one's life for one's friends."[180]

This commandment to love is not a new command. It is what Jesus identified as the foundational principle upon which the law and the prophets are built:

"'You shall love the Lord your God with all your heart, and with all your soul, and with all your mind.' This is the greatest and first commandment. And a second is like it: 'You shall love your neighbor as yourself.' On these two commandments hang all the law and the prophets."[181]

---

[179] Matthew 28:18-20.
[180] John 15:12-13.
[181] Matthew 22:37:39, Mark 12:30-31, Luke 10:26-40.

And so our mission is consistent with Jesus' mission: to love in a sacrificial way by laying down our lives for the sake of others.

This kind of love changes our perceptions of reality.

This kind of love brings about a new kind of reality.

This kind of love is what brought Jesus here in the first place:

"For God so loved the world that he gave his only Son, so that everyone who believes in him may not perish but may have eternal life."[182]

This scripture, likely one of the most famous in all the Bible, tells us God loves us and through Jesus loves us into a new reality...an eternal reality...a reality in which our primary mission is to love God and love our neighbors.

We call this eternal reality...the new kingdom.

Divided We Fail

In the Church today, we oftentimes find ourselves divided into two camps. Some of us are proclaimers of the truth of Christ through thoughtful presentations of the Gospel, while others of us attempt to live in the way of Christ, dedicating our efforts to the betterment of those less fortunate (aka social justice issues). Both of these are good and both of these are necessary. But, when we promote one without the other, we are like fingers without opposing thumbs; unable to fully grasp the tools necessary to build the new kingdom we are called to

---

[182] John 3:16.

construct. The degree to which we are guilty of this is the degree to which we fail to remain true to the mission Jesus placed before us and are participants in the Great Omission rather than the Great Commission...omission of a half that makes a whole.

Proclamation does not ring true apart from those whose hands are dirtied in the service of others. And, social justice is not truly *just* when it is enacted apart from the *truth*. The first is the *truth* without the *way* and the second is the *way* without the *truth*. Apart from one another they can never lead to an abundant *life*. Therefore what is truly *just* and *true* is a *both/and* manifestation of the kingdom...a place in which both the *truth* and *way* of Jesus make visible a new kingdom *life*.

As followers of Jesus, we must proclaim *and* demonstrate. Our proclamation announces the truth while our demonstration authenticates the truth of our proclamation. When we demonstrate without proclamation we make things better today without concern for the future, and when we proclaim without demonstration we ignore the wounded around us and deliver only a hope for a better tomorrow.

Proclamation *and* demonstration...

This is the way of Jesus, and as such it should be our way as well.

The Way

If as Jesus' disciples we are willing to acknowledge Jesus as the manifestation of the *way*, then we must also be willing to accept that this *way* of Jesus leads us up a mountain and to a cross:

> *"Then Jesus told his disciples, 'If any want to become my followers, let them deny themselves and take up their cross and follow me. For those who want to save their life will lose it, and those who lose their life for my sake will find it.'"*[183]

Everything in history changes at the cross. "The cross is not a detour or a hurdle on the way to the kingdom, nor is it even the way to the kingdom; it is the kingdom come."[184] And so, it is at the cross that we come face to face with the way in which we follow Jesus, a way that includes a sacrifice. In our case we get to take a pass on the horrendous sacrifice on the cross, however we must nonetheless undergo a sacrificial death that for many of us proves equally challenging: we must embrace the death of our self and self-interest.

The degree to which we struggle with self-interest is revealed in the degree to which we lean upon proclamation over and above demonstration. In proclamation we stay relatively safe for we risk very little other than perhaps loss of social standing in groups where we consider social standing to be more important than standing with Jesus. A proclamation only gospel is an adaptive behavior that delays our need to do the harder work of demonstration. But in demonstration, we must stand alongside Jesus, putting others needs above our own, giving of ourselves in ways that perhaps brings their pain into our lives. Self-sacrifice in any form is costly and should we

---

[183] Matthew 16:24-25, Mark 8:34-35.
[184] Yoder, *The Politics of Jesus*, 51.

ever doubt that, all we need do is turn our eyes in the direction of the cross.

What Do We Really Believe?

In his book *Insurrection*, Peter Rollins suggests "the truth of a person is to be located, not in the story they tell about themselves, but in the drives and desires that manifest themselves in material practices."[185] In other words, when our actions fall short of the beliefs we claim to embrace, these actions actually reveal our true beliefs.

• When we claim loving our neighbor as something we believe and yet do not do it, we actually reveal the truth that we do not really love our neighbor.

• When we claim to care about people who are hungry and yet do not engage in feeding them, we actually reveal the truth that we do not really care about hungry people.

•When we claim to be concerned for the homeless in our community and yet do not aid in providing them shelter, we actually reveal the truth that we do not really care about homeless people.

In other words, the beliefs we claim to embrace are not supported or revealed by our behaviors.

Oftentimes we attempt to assuage our conscience in these matters by attending church and claiming to be a Christian in order to present an image of ourselves as one who loves God and loves our neighbor, but in actuality we are actors playing

---

[185] Peter Rollins, *Insurrection* (Nashville, Tenn.: Howard Books, 2011), 92.

roles who leave the ecclesial stage to resume our real lives...lives that exist at some distance from the *way* that makes those *truths* of Jesus evident. We are, in essence, embracing Jesus *lite*, a Jesus without the burden of the cross which is no Jesus at all.

A False Gospel

Now, the thing that should cause us some degree of concern about this partial gospel we seem so willing to embrace is this: when we are not proclaiming the full gospel...the triune gospel of the *way*, the *truth* and the *life*...we are in fact proclaiming a false gospel...a false gospel that only partially reveals the new kingdom Jesus proclaimed.

Therefore, when we find our message and our lives the subject of cultural ridicule and mockery, when we see research that points to a decline of the Church in the Western world, and when we find ourselves engaging in adaptive strategies rather than walking with Jesus, we can assume it is this false gospel, this Jesus *lite* that is failing to inspire and change the world.

Count the Cost

Jesus never told the disciples it would be easy. He never said all they needed to do was explain the Good News or invite others into it; quite the contrary. Oftentimes Jesus spoke of the cost that came with following Him seemingly as a way to possibly discourage the marginally committed from embarking down this path:

> *"Whoever comes to me and does not hate father and mother, wife and children, brothers and sisters, yes, and even life itself, cannot be my disciple. Whoever does not carry the cross and follow me cannot be my disciple."*[186]

Cross carrying is hard. Cross carrying is messy business for cross carrying locates us on the path of Jesus as we attempt to engage the world on His terms and not ours. Cross carrying produces kingdom fruit and as followers of Jesus we are to be co-laborers in the harvest. However, a lack of this fruit in our lives comes with certain disincentives, as we shall see in the parable of the fig tree:

> *On the following day, when they came from Bethany, he was hungry. Seeing in the distance a fig tree in leaf, he went to see whether perhaps he would find anything on it. When he came to it, he found nothing but leaves, for it was not the season for figs. He said to it, "May no one ever eat fruit from you again."*[187]

Later in the story, Jesus and the disciples passed by the fig tree again and saw that it had indeed *"withered away to its roots."*[188] The fig tree's purpose was to produce fruit. Without fruit, it had no purpose and so its life was taken away. The purpose of a disciple is also to produce fruit. Without fruit the disciple has no place in the kingdom. So not living a kingdom life in its fullness places us in a rather precarious position…a position the religious leaders of Jesus' time found themselves in as well:

---

[186] Luke 14:26-27.
[187] Mark 11:12-14.
[188] Mark 11:19-20.

> "*But woe to you, scribes and Pharisees, hypocrites! For you lock people out of the kingdom of heaven. For you do not go in yourselves, and when others are going in, you stop them.*"[189]

So whenever we as "little Christs" (Christians) do not go *all in* by embracing *all three* attributes of Jesus...the *way*, the *truth*, and the *life*...we not only do not enter the Kingdom ourselves, but we prevent others from entering as well. To the degree that we are guilty of this, Jesus casts "woe" upon us. According to the Merriam-Webster dictionary, the word "woe" means "a condition of deep suffering from misfortune, affliction, or grief." This is a condition I know I would prefer to avoid and I assume you would as well.

We have another indicator of how much Jesus frowns upon those who diminish or inhibit those who are being drawn into the Kingdom:

> "*If any of you put a stumbling block before one of these little ones who believe in me, it would be better for you if a great millstone were hung around your neck and you were thrown into the sea.*"[190]

Again, none of us wants to find ourselves in that position. And yet, in our presentation of Jesus *lite* we come dangerously close to that neckwear.

Sermon on the Mount

If we wanted to find a summary of Jesus' teachings on life in the new kingdom, we would be hard pressed to find a better

---

[189] Matthew 23:13.
[190] Matthew 18:6, Mark 9:42, Luke 17:1-2.

one than the Sermon on the Mount. This revolutionary text begins by telling us *"When Jesus saw the crowds, he went up the mountain; and after he sat down, his disciples came to him."*[191] An alternative description of the Sermon location is presented in Luke; *"And he came down with them and stood on a level place, with a great multitude of people."*[192] This discrepancy of location is not nearly as important as the common theme of an ascent or descent from up on high, for the location of the story "is not geographical but theological...the mountain of revelation."[193]

Ok. It's time to think semiotically again. Going up or coming down from the mountain is neither here nor there for both are signs, signs that connect Jesus to Moses for we know Moses went up to the mountaintop to be with God and then came down from the mountaintop as the bearer of God's message for his people. However, the signifiers depart company here because Moses spoke on behalf of God and Jesus spoke in his own voice and in his own name.[194] And, in his speaking, he radicalized[195] that which Moses came down from the mountain to present.

The first words of the Sermon are *"Blessed are the poor in spirit, for theirs is the kingdom of heaven."*[196] From here, Jesus proceeds to challenge the prevailing cultural concept of what it means to be blessed or happy. "Now it is the wretched who are first in line for God's abundant blessings, reflecting the overall reversal brought about by God's liberation of the world."[197]

---

[191] Matthew 5:1.
[192] Luke 6:17.
[193] Eugene Boring, *The New Interpreter's Bible*, ed. Leander Keck (Nashville: Abingdon Press, ©1994-2004), 8:175.
[194] David E. Garland, *Reading Matthew: A Literary and Theological Commentary*, Reading the New Testament Series (Macon, Ga.: Smyth & Helwys Pub., ©2001), 53.
[195] Boring, *The New Interpreter's Bible*, 8:189.
[196] Matthew 5:3.

This new happiness "reverses all human values; happiness is no longer attached to wealth, to having enough, to good reputation, power, possessions of the goods of this world."[198] The Sermon on the Mount is a manifesto of new kingdom living...a manifesto for the new creation Jesus is speaking into existence.

Just as God spoke original creation into existence, Jesus now speaks New Creation into existence. The truths of this New Creation speak not only to external condition but also to inward consequence. They declare happiness (blessedness) is no longer dependent on external or physical conditions but instead happiness in *life* is rooted in the *way* and *truth* of Jesus' new kingdom.

After redefining what it means to be *blessed*, the manifesto then turns its attention toward those who are the *blessed* ones. To do this, Jesus uses images of *salt* and *light* to illustrate his point:

> *"You are the salt of the earth; but if salt has lost its taste, how can its saltiness be restored? It is no longer good for anything, but is thrown out and trampled under foot."*[199]

The verb μωρανθῇ or mOranthE, translated here as *lost its taste* can also be translated as "becomes foolish."[200] As such, we can read the text to say those who are blessed in this new kingdom are the wise ones, the ones who embrace and live out

---

[197] Katharine Sakenfield, ed., *The New Interpreter's Dictionary of the Bible*. (Nashville, TN: Abingdon Press, 2006), 734.
[198] Ernest, James D., *Theological lexicon of the New Testament*. (Peabody, MA: Hendrickson Publishers, 1994), 438
[199] Matthew 5:13.
[200] R.T. France, *The Gospel According to Matthew*. (Grand Rapids: Wm. B. Eerdman Publishing Company, 1985), 175.

this new kingdom life. But if you become foolish instead, and do not embrace this new kingdom life, you will be thrown out and trampled upon, no longer good for anything.

Jesus continued with light as a metaphor for the blessed ones:

> *"You are the light of the world. A city built on a hill cannot be hid. No one after lighting a lamp puts it under the bushel basket, but on the lamp stand, and it gives light to all in the house. In the same way, let your light shine before others, so that they may see your good works and give glory to your Father in heaven."*[201]

Light illuminates and drives out the darkness, light also keeps us from stumbling or falling victim to unforeseen dangers, but light also has another purpose: "to let things be seen as they are."[202] Once the reality of this world is illuminated and the desperateness of our situation apart from God is understood, our purpose as Christians and the Church is to live in a way that fills the world with God-light…light that reveals the *way*, the *truth* and the *life* of the new kingdom. God's first proclamation in original creation was "Let there be light,"[203] God's covenant with Noah was also a light covenant…a rainbow,[204] and now in the New Creation, Jesus calls us…his Church…to be the *light of the world*.[205]

---

[201] Matthew 5:14-16
[202] Boring, *The New Interpreter's Bible*, 8:182.
[203] Genesis 1:3.
[204] Genesis 9:1-17.
[205] Matthew 5:14.

Which New Normal?

Based upon our patient history, our diagnostic testing, and our review of the literature, we need to consider the options. Is our patient (the Church) at the point we need to just accept its condition and downward trajectory as the new normal and simply try our best to provide for its needs and keep it comfortable in its final years? Or, does our Church have the collective strength to embrace an alternate new normal, one in which it re-connects the *truth* of Jesus with the *way* of Jesus so it might abandon the life support systems, choosing instead a new normal we can truly live with?

If your choice is to embrace the first option…the gradual, slow death of the church, you can stop reading here. Go lay down. Save your strength. You are going to need it.

However, for those of us who choose to embrace the second option… the option that leads to resurrection, let's talk about some ways in which we might reconnect the *way* of Christ with the *truth* of Christ that will breathe the breath of *life* into our faith and our dusty Church.

Part 4 - Treatment Plan

Chapter 7 – Rehabilitation

Diagnostic Strategy: Developing a Treatment Plan

If you are still reading, you must have chosen the second option. Congratulations! A willingness to continue is a critical element in the rehabilitation of any patient. However, before we consider potential options for our Church, let's discuss some possible rehabilitative strategies appropriate to the patient examples we discussed earlier.

Hearing Loss

When a mild to moderate hearing loss is diagnosed and confirmed, hearing aids can be utilized to restore the patient's ability to hear in most situations. Even those patients with a severe to profound sensorineural hearing loss are no longer without hope for under certain conditions they too can have some degree of hearing restored via a device called a cochlear implant. These implants involve the insertion of electrodes into the cochlea and the wearing of a receiver that is held in place on the scalp with a magnet…pretty amazing.

Obesity

Obesity comes with its own set of challenges. Causes can be both medical and/or psychological, but if the patient is willing to contribute their best efforts to the weight loss program, the results can be amazing.

Dizziness

Dizziness is often complicated in that multiple system failures can contribute to the patient finding him or herself unable to negotiate familiar landscapes. Fortunately, functionality can oftentimes be improved through medical interventions or therapeutic strategies that retrain the balance system to compensate for damaged or declining biology.

Loss of Memory

Failing memory is a symptom of a variety of conditions. Some of these can be addressed through pharmacological interventions while others may require the addition of therapy as a means to maintain heightened functionality as long as possible. Early diagnosis and intervention is key to positive outcomes as is the willing participation of the patient.

Pain

Pain, the physiological alarm system for our bodies, serves as a way to expedite our pursuit of positive alternatives in its own special way. Unfortunately, many of the avenues open to us in the area of pain alleviation do not work toward addressing the cause of the pain but instead only serve to numb ourselves to that which is calling us to action. Either way, pain causes things to happen.

Moving Forward

Now granted, many of our patient examples are symptoms of an inevitable decline that all of us must embrace one day. However, as the Church, our decline is in no way inevitable or necessary. In fact, while our eternal kingdom destination is clear, the way in which we engage the distance between here and then remains somewhat up for grabs.

And so, as ecclesial diagnosticians, we have thus far been able to paint a clear picture of not only our current situation, but also of how we got here, and the ways in which our adaptive strategies are working counter to our best interests.

Now, we must offer up a treatment plan that discourages us from accepting our present condition as the *new normal* and points us toward a *new normal we can live with*.

For our patient, the Church, we need to place before ourselves a goal: a vision of our destination: a place where our *beliefs* are made evident by our *behaviors* and our *behaviors* provide evidence of those *beliefs*: a place where our *demonstration* reinforces our *proclamation* and our *proclamation* points to Jesus as the *way* and the *truth* that makes *life* possible: a place where we become those disciples who bring a little kingdom living to this earth. And so, in the next few pages, we will do just that as we imagine a world of possibilities.

The topics that follow are not intended to be all-inclusive, nor is our purpose here to elevate these specific needs above others in the cornucopia of opportunities that exist in our world. However, they are intended to act as conversation starters…to inspire some of us to action…and hopefully to point our Church in a direction that more honestly honors its Christological inspiration.

> "Some things are not an answer; they're a start. And sometimes we need starts more than we need answers: baby steps in the right direction."[206]

---

[206] Leonard I. Sweet, *The Well-Played Life: Why Pleasing God Doesn't Have to Be Such Hard Work* (Carol Stream, IL: Tyndale House Publishers, Inc., 2014), 102.

So let's take some baby steps...some first steps in the direction of our becoming a church more like the church Jesus was dying to create.

Healthcare

The Church, of which we are a part, has a long history in the area of health care. History tells us during the epidemic of the second century known as the Plague of Galen (165-180 AD) in which hundreds of thousands literally died in the streets, Christians distinguished themselves from their contemporaries by caring for those who were sick in spite of the risks.[207]

• They stayed when others fled.

• They touched the untouchables when the majority would not come near.

• They cared for the sick when a caring presence was not just hard to find, but essential for survival.

"Their acts of mercy extended to all the suffering regardless of class, tribe, or religion and created conditions in which others accepted their faith"[208] as their own. In essence, the Christians did "risky, compelling, and good things that helped people."[209] Resultantly, their behaviors provided evidence of their beliefs as their actions spoke louder than their words.

Once Christianity became legal under the reign of Constantine, "Gregory of Nyssa's brother, Bishop Basil,

---

[207] Bass, *A People's History of Christianity*, 59.
[208] Ibid., 60.
[209] Ibid.

averted a disaster in Cappadocia during a famine in 368 AD when he used nearly all his family's fortune to feed the poor through the creation of an ancient food bank[210] of sorts. He also built one of the very first Christian hospitals in addition to a hospice to care for the dying.[211] Today this tradition continues in that we have a variety of religious based hospitals throughout the country that are enabled and supported by various denominations. Now you might say your church participates in that presence through the finances you provide to these denominational endeavors, and you would be correct, but what about more local and hands-on opportunities that would enable your church to more actively participate in this aspect of kingdom work?

On a local level, we see instances of kingdom care exhibited in a variety of ways. Some churches make space available in their facilities for free weekly health clinics while others work alongside medical missions organizations in an effort to bring affordable, if not free health care to those of greatest need within the community.[212]

Recently, I had the opportunity to speak with Todd Littleton, pastor of Snow Hill Baptist Church, in Tuttle, Oklahoma where they have been engaged in a monthly free clinic to serve their community for about four years. The church provides the space and volunteers for the clinic, which includes a physician, physician's assistant, nurse, and pharmacist. Non-medical members of the church participate in administrative functions in support of the clinic. Todd told me,

---

[210] Ibid., 63.
[211] Ibid.
[212] http://www.goodsamaritanhealth.org

"We were told two of the largest chronic care issues were hypertension and diabetes. We have found this to be true. While we help with other needs, of course, these tend to be the needs of our returning patients."[213]

Now, you might say your church is not big enough or it lacks the resources necessary to engage in this sort of medical mission. However, before you do, you should consider that Tuttle is a town of approximately 6000 people. What is needed over and above resources is a vision of the kingdom. With this vision, resources become available. As such, Snow Hill is a vibrant example of how a church of any size can engage in a bit of kingdom care in its local community.

However, if you do not feel called to engage in health care at this level, a variety of opportunities exist if you will just think a step or two outside the box. Perhaps in your particular context you do not have people who can enable a clinic such as the one at Snow Hill. Instead, you could subsidize office space for a doctor in an underserved area or perhaps even negotiate with local doctors to see patients on a limited basis at a reduced rate with your church contributing financially to these efforts. The possibility also exists to supplement a doctor's salary so they are able to provide a certain amount of free medical care for patients within your community. Once you start thinking along these lines, opportunities that once seemed out of reach will no longer lie beyond your grasp.

---

[213] email conversation 3/10/2014

Abortion

While this topic falls under the heading of health care, its importance demands dedicated consideration for nowhere is the battle between the church and the culture more contentious than on the topic of abortion. While there are faith based organizations whose purpose is to provide services and counseling to those who find themselves in the midst of an unwanted or crisis pregnancy, the more visible efforts of the Church in the United States ultimately revolve around attempts to overturn Rowe v. Wade. While these efforts arise out of noble ambitions, we can in no way claim they are diminishing demand for abortions based upon the research published by CDC in 2010 stating 765,651 legal abortions were reported to their agency.[214] That is approximately 87 abortions per hour of every day of every month of the year. In fact, the New York Times reported in 2011 that the average number of abortions in that city has "averaged 90,000 in recent years, or about 40 percent of all pregnancies, twice the national rate."[215] Let me say that again…40% of all pregnancies in New York end in abortion. By any measure, abortion is clearly becoming a choice many have no trouble making as we are aborting almost 20% of those destined to become future citizens in our nation.[216] As such, we must admit our efforts to change the conscience and actions of our country through political engagement have fallen woefully short.

Before anyone laments the apparent failure of political strategies to reduce access to legal abortions, let's pause here

---

[214] http://www.cdc.gov/reproductivehealth/data_stats/
[215] http://www.nytimes.com/2011/01/07/nyregion/07abortion.html?_r=0
[216] http://www.census.gov/compendia/statab/2012/tables/12s0078.pdf

for a moment to consider what would be different if Rowe v. Wade were overturned. Would the demand for abortion go away? Not likely. Instead it would just move underground placing both mother and child in a position of greater risk. As a Christian community I cannot help but think our efforts would be better invested if we were to follow an alternative strategy.

In the history of our faith, the reliance on laws to change the hearts and minds of God's people met with little success. Jesus did not offer legal strategies to change the world; instead Jesus offered heart transplants - the implantation of a caring heart over and above a model for change that centered on political engagement. For better and perhaps more effective ways to protect the most vulnerable in our midst, we need to look to Jesus for inspiration.

In Jesus, we saw one who walked alongside others in their greatest time of need, serving as an advocate for those who found themselves the object of societal scorn. In doing so He offered forgiveness and hope to those confronted with the most difficult decisions of their lives. If our calling is to follow Jesus, then perhaps the needs of those we seek to protect are better served by our standing alongside the pregnant mothers who see abortion as their best or only solution rather than standing in front of the door to the abortion clinic preventing their entry.

Now, by standing alongside a mother who is pregnant and scared I do not in any way mean to suggest we support a decision that ultimately leads to the taking of one life and the scarring of another for a life time. Instead, I suggest we inspire these reluctant mothers with alternatives that avoid the tragic outcomes so readily available in our society.

To do this, we must first change our attitudes concerning what typically comes across as a condemnation of those who find themselves pregnant and alone. This only serves to reinforce the public shame that is oftentimes pronounced upon them prompting many parents to encourage their daughters to get an abortion rather than "ruin" their lives with a very public acknowledgement of their situation.[217] "Ironically, such an attitude assumes that individual sexual conduct is more significant than a community's willingness to receive its children."[218] We must be willing to receive our pregnant sisters and daughters into the loving arms of a community which while not condoning or supporting the actions that located them in this situation, none-the-less embraces and walks alongside them to support alternatives to society's apparent easy way out.

> "We must be a people who stand ready to receive and care for any child, not just as if it were one of ours, but because in fact each is one of ours."[219]

As the story goes, Jesus was teaching in the temple when a group of Pharisees brought before him a woman caught in the act of adultery. The Pharisees were attempting to trap Jesus into saying something against the Law of Moses, which taught such women should be stoned to death. After a curious pause in which Jesus was said to be writing in the dirt, Jesus announced his decision for all to hear: *"Let anyone among you who is without sin be the first to throw a stone at her."*[220] In what we can imagine was a moment of not only great disappointment, but

---

[217] Hauerwas, *A Community of Character*, 208.
[218] Ibid.
[219] Ibid., 229.
[220] John 8:7.

somber reflection, each of the accusers, one by one, walked away. Jesus then asked the woman, *"Woman, where are they? Has no one condemned you?"*[221] She answered no, to which Jesus replied, *"Neither do I condemn you. Go your way, and from now on do not sin again."*[222]

This story reveals one of the most powerful acts of redemption in the New Testament for in it Jesus did not advantage himself as one who was greater than this woman who had been caught in a deadly sin. Instead, he lowered himself to look her in the eye, offering forgiveness...forgiveness that is available to everyone, not just those who seemingly maintain or enforce the Law.

The politics of our legal adaptive strategy on this issue have unfortunately placed the church in a position similar to that of the Pharisees...a position from which we stand with rocks at the ready...offering judgment and condemnation over and above the true "rock" of our salvation. Not only has this strategy met with only limited success in the political arena, but it has created a cultural divide across which neither side even understands the language of the other any longer. Rather than continue to excavate this chasm through ongoing legal strategies, as followers of Christ, it seems a more appropriate strategy would be to embrace a posture faithful to the position of Jesus...lowered to the level of the frightened and accused so she can look directly into the eyes of Jesus...the eyes of forgiveness and hope for a future that seems desperately out of her control and beyond the reach of her present reality.

---

[221] John 8:10.
[222] John 8:11.

We begin to manifest this reality by providing alternatives that point to "yes" rather than engage in a strategy that revolves around a "no." When we align ourselves with "no" over and above "yes" we become part of a problem that only points to the solution we are trying to prevent. "No" doesn't provide alternatives. "No" just stands in the way. We become a people of "yes" when our options enable our daughters and sisters to feel equally valued alongside our concern for the unborn.

To do this the church may have to become the home a girl in crises can no longer return to. We may need to provide prenatal counseling and supplies, trips to the doctor's office, food and shelter, as well as a hand to hold during the birthing classes. We may need to serve as a resource to find loving parents should the mother not be able to care for her child. We may have to continue to provide for mother and child as mom learns new skills that will enable her to care for and nurture this new addition to her life. In essence, we need to become those who love both the unborn child *and* the reluctant mother. We need to love them into the kingdom of God rather than push them away. If we were to manifest Christ in this manner, it is not hard to imagine the number of abortions in this country would decline along with the number of practitioners willing to provide abortion services.

As the Church, we also need to provide support, love and encouragement to those who have chosen to abort their unborn children rather than assume the stance of the Pharisees sentencing them to a death by exclusion from a loving community of fellow sinners. Ultimately, those who love must also be willing to walk alongside the women who see no way out of their situation other than abortion...even if this means walking with them through the clinic doors and providing them a ride home and a hand to hold in the emptiness of the moments that will follow. In doing this, we in no way condone their actions, but instead we echo the forgiving words that Jesus uttered in his most desperate of moments on behalf of those who orchestrated his execution: *"Father, forgive them; for they know not what they do."*[223]

Widows

"Religion that is pure and undefiled before God, the Father, is this: to care for orphans and widows in their distress."[224]

In ancient Israel, after the death of a woman's husband, responsibility for her care fell upon her sons.[225] If she was still of childbearing age and without sons, it became her father-in-law's responsibly to arrange a marriage for her.[226] As a result, if she were widowed beyond childbearing years and without sons to provide for her, she found herself in a rather precarious position.[227] The book of Acts tells a story of those who found themselves in this position when a dispute arose over what

---

[223] Luke 23:34 (KJV).
[224] James 1:27.
[225] M. Cathleen Kaveny, "The Order of Widows: What the Early Church Can Teach Us About Older Women and Health Care", *Christian Bioethics: Non-Ecumenical Studies in Medical Morality* 11, no. 1 (2005): 13.
[226] Ibid.
[227] Ibid.

some apparently felt was the preferential treatment of Hebrew widows over and above the Hellenist ones.[228]

> "Now during those days, when the disciples were increasing in number, the Hellenists complained against the Hebrews because their widows were being neglected in the daily distribution of food."[229]

In an effort to find a solution to this dilemma, the disciples gathered together and chose Stephen, along with six others to make sure *all* the widows in the care of the Church received proper treatment.[230] This tradition of caring for widows continued in the Church as evidence suggests by the middle of the third century, the Church in Rome was caring for some fifteen hundred widows and poor people.[231]

For those of us who have experienced the challenges associated with caring for aging parents, we are familiar with how the current reality of our faith community resides at some distance from this ancient example. This deficiency is at least partially encouraged by the age related segregationist strategies that exist within churches.

For an example of these segregationist tendencies we need look no further than Sunday mornings for as soon as we enter the door of our church, we begin to split off from one another.

---

[228] The Hebrews were Christians converts who were living and raised in Israel. The Hellenists were Jewish converts who had returned to Judea and not only spoke Greek but had adopted certain practices of Greek culture.
http://www.bibleversestudy.com/acts/acts6-hellenists.htm
[229] Acts 6:1.
[230] Acts 6:5.
[231] Peter Brown, *Lectures On the History of Religions*, vol. 13, *The Body and Society: Men, Women, and Sexual Renunciation in Early Christianity* (New York: Columbia University Press, 1988), 148.

There are places for infants, toddlers, elementary age children, middle schoolers, high schoolers, college students, singles, young marrieds, seniors, etc. Even though this segregation is done in the name of providing better services to the target group, in the end, these misdirected efforts rob each group of the benefit of learning from and engaging in a cross-generational manner. As a way to better understand the insanity of this strategy, let's lay this template for disengagement on top of another scenario: a night out with the family.

Suppose you and your family were planning on going out for dinner. You weighed the various options for where you wanted to go and ultimately you selected a restaurant in the area known as *family friendly* since you have a 2 year old, a 14 year old, one in college, and a grandmother and grandfather who will all be joining you for dinner this evening. Then suppose as you entered this *family friendly* restaurant your group was split up and directed to age appropriate areas: one area where your 2 year old could dine age appropriately, one area where your 14 year old could do the same, another area where those of college age gathered to dine, and one nice and quite area where your parents could eat their dinner in peace, leaving you and your spouse to enjoy the evening with the other parents dining in the restaurant.

It doesn't make much sense does it? But in the typical church, that is exactly what we do each and every week. People arrive at church as a family, and then we split them apart and direct them to areas better able to meet their "individual" needs. When it comes to age in the church, we are aggressively segregationists. While this strategy aligns with our individualistic cultural predispositions it runs counter to the Biblical narrative that informs us we are one body in desperate need of one another.[232]

In the area of community and cross-generational care, our efforts will be better aligned with our original call when we stop fracturing the Body of Christ along age related boundaries that limit our capacity for meaningful relationships within the Church. These segregationist strategies are short-sighted and tend to diminish our community rather than enrich it as all ages would be better served by our gathering around a common table whether we are able to feed ourselves or not. It is also reasonable to assume our continuing to engage the elder members of the community in ways that are appropriate to their abilities not only enriches the community as a whole, but also provides them with social stimulation that ultimately delays the need for more specialized care.

This is not to say there does not come a time in which needs can outweigh the ability of the family or community to provide for the aging among us, but it does suggest the church falls woefully short in the ways in which we encourage the family and support those who find themselves at the end of life's journey.

When the need for specialized care ultimately arises, the church should be at the forefront of eldercare by creating and supporting care homes in which those approaching the end of their journey are comfortable and cared for within a Christian community whose involvement consists of more than dropping by on Sundays for a church service or wandering the halls at

---

[232] 1 Corinthians 12.

Christmas time singing carols and handing out store-bought candy canes.

In any event, a little brainstorming on the part of the church will no doubt reveal a variety of ways in which your church can better enable community while at the same time providing support to the aging in our midst and their families.

Orphans

Research tells us there are 400,000 children currently in the foster care system in the United States with 100,000 of those in need of a permanent home.[233] While many of those who foster and seek to adopt children are indeed Christians, these statistics show us, we still have hundreds of thousands of opportunities to manifest a religion *pure* and *undefiled* in this area. As a way to increase the efforts of the church in the area of orphan care, there are several things we can do.

First of all, we can begin by defining our churches as communities where those who provide homes for these little ones are celebrated. We do this by telling their stories, by actively working on behalf of those considering adopting a child, and by partnering with these adoptive children and families on their journey. This partnering may take the form of financial support, childcare, diapers, or any number of things parents need when adding a little one to their family. But most of all, we must be willing to walk alongside these families, doing everything we can to insure the success of both parent and child as members of a loving community of faith.

---

[233] http://www.adoption.org/adopt/child-adoption-statistics.php

The story of Christianity is a story of adoption, for we were all lost, then found and adopted into the family of God. Therefore, as God's adopted ones, we should be celebrators of adoption as a way to do unto others, that which has been done unto us.[234] For those wanting more information on adoption or looking for ways to connect your church with others around the country working to make sure all of our young ones have a home, you can visit the Christian Alliance for Orphans website.[235]

Hunger

Feeding the hungry is an area in which many churches and non-profits are quite active. Food is donated and prepared and then distributed to those willing to come to the distribution point to get their free meal. Ultimately, these are noble efforts that attempt to address a growing problem in this country and around the world, but our strategies in this area are similar to what we found in our medical investigations earlier. Oftentimes, we tend to address the symptoms rather than dealing with the real problem. Being hungry is a symptom of something else…something like unemployment, homelessness, or poverty for example. Hunger does not cause homelessness, unemployment, or poverty. Hunger is a symptom of these conditions, and as such, many of our efforts in this area are adaptive strategies that address the symptoms rather than solutions to the underlying cause. There is a pain (hunger) and we provide something to help alleviate that pain (food), but this will not make the pain go away. In fact, it allows and perhaps

---

[234] Luke 6:31, Matthew 7:12.
[235] http://www.christianalliancefororphans.org/

encourages the condition to get worse as we get dependent on the painkiller (free food) rather than addressing the underlying cause.

One of the books that really brought this issue into better focus for me was Bob Lupton's *Toxic Charity*. Bob has years of experience in this area and is the founder and president of Focused Community Strategies in Atlanta. He states that in his experience "our free food and clothing distribution encourages ever-growing handout lines, diminishing the dignity of the poor while increasing their dependency."[236] He goes on to further say that our "giving to those in need what they could be gaining from their own initiative may well be the kindest way to destroy people."[237] Ouch.

The typical efforts of the church in the area of food distribution also tend to divide by creating an *"us* vs. *them"* situation. We, as the good, privileged, and resourced people are there to help the poor and destitute. Our efforts allow us to feel good about ourselves while at the same time unintentionally diminishing their chances of self-respect and esteem for their humanity. Granted, the clients of the standard food distribution charity receive a benefit, but in the end, they typically return to their life situation with a bit of food and we are able to go back home feeling good about our lot in life. Now before you take issue with what appears to be the disgruntled ramblings of a cynic, let's look a little deeper at the issue.

In his book, Lupton identifies the consequences giveaway programs typically have on those who seek out these services:[238]

---

[236] Robert D. Lupton, *Toxic Charity: How Churches and Charities Hurt Those They Help (and How to Reverse It)* (New York: HarperOne, 2012), 4.
[237] Ibid.

- Give once and you elicit appreciation.
- Give twice and you create anticipation.
- Give three times and you create expectation.
- Give four times and it becomes entitlement.
- Give five times and you establish dependency.

In many cases, this dependency is a two way street. The poor become dependent on the distribution of goods that flow out of our abundance, and we, to some degree, become dependent on them as a means to salve the guilt we feel for this abundance. They need us and we need them, but the problem is, they are ultimately diminished while we in contrast are encouraged and empowered.

Granted, there are times when giving at the moment of crisis is appropriate, but outside of a crisis state, we should pursue other ways in which our efforts help move people toward self-sufficiency, empowerment, and at the very least a restoration of the self-esteem and humanity of those we seek to serve.

Most of us are familiar with the story of Jesus feeding the 5000...of how 2 fish and 5 loaves of bread became enough food to feed them all with leftovers.[239] It is truly a miraculous story, but the story does not end there, for afterward Jesus traveled across the lake and was again surrounded by a large crowd. Jesus revealed their intentions:

---

[238] Ibid., 130.
[239] John 6:9-13.

> *"Very truly, I tell you, you are looking for me, not because you saw signs, but because you ate your fill of the loaves."*[240]

I like how the Message paraphrases this text:

> *"You've come looking for me not because you saw God in my actions but because I fed you, filled your stomachs - and for free."*[241]

Therein lies the problem. Even when in the presence of Jesus, the Son of God, God in the flesh, people were still people, and quite willing to let someone do for them what they could do for themselves. Lupton's progression to dependency seems to ring as true then as it does today.

As an alternative to the normal way in which we approach food charity, Lupton suggests an alternative. He proposes rather than food giveaway programs, churches encourage and develop food co-op programs. He uses the Georgia Avenue Food Co-op as an example. Rather than give away food to all comers, those in need of food must join the co-op, which requires they make not only a financial investment but also an investment of their personal time and energies. In the case of the Georgia Avenue Food Co-op, the monetary commitment amounts to a semi-weekly fee of $3, which the co-op leverages into $30 worth of food. "Over time co-op members build friendships, share meals, listen to one another's joys and woes, pray for one another - in essence they become a church."[242] Everyone who is a member of the co-op is involved. "Some make the run to the food bank. Others do set up. Some sort

---

[240] John 6:26.
[241] John 6:26 (MSG).
[242] Lupton, *Toxic Charity*, 53.

and box. Still others are assigned to cleanup duty... [And some] deliver a box to a shut-in member."[243]

He says (and I agree), "we have to find a way for outsiders to become insiders. Recipients must become dispensers, authors of the rules, builders of community."[244] Otherwise, the relationships spawned by food giveaway programs become adversarial and foster dependency that perpetuates an *"us vs. them"* mentality.

Food co-ops are not the only option available to the Church...especially suburban churches for most of them have more land than is currently being occupied by buildings and parking lots. Rather than allow it to sit idle, it could instead become an opportunity for the church to build greater community while at the same time coming to the aid of those who find themselves without enough food by implementing what is coming to be known as a community garden. In addition, if those in need of food are located in relative proximity to the church garden, they can be invited to exchange their labors for the food they receive...perhaps even contributing time and effort to the gardens of others. In any event, a strategy such as this works toward multiple ends: food is provided, relationships are enabled, and the kingdom is restored as we tend the garden.[245] Also, neighbors of the church could in essence "lease" garden plots in exchange for donating a portion of their food to the food program. Again, the food charity becomes food production as those in the community work alongside one another for the greater good.

---

[243] Ibid.
[244] Ibid, 62.
[245] Genesis 2:15.

What a wonderful visible demonstration to the community! Whenever anyone drives past the church they are going to see a living manifestation of the kingdom, a place where beliefs and behaviors truly become one.

Be prepared however, for these efforts oftentimes come with an unexpected cost. A friend of mine, Dottie Escobedo-Frank, who at the time was pastor of Crossroads United Methodist Church in Phoenix found herself and her church in the crosshairs of community scorn when their efforts to care for the homeless resulted in the surrounding neighborhood attempting to put an end to the these efforts because it was bringing *those kind of people* into the neighborhood. When we become an outpost that manifests kingdom living, we oftentimes uncover resistance in unexpected places.

Homelessness

Here are the current statistics on homelessness in the United States according to the National Alliance to End Homelessness:[246]

• There are 633,782 people experiencing homelessness on any given night in the United States.

• Of that number, 239,403 are people in families, and 392,945 are individuals.

• Slightly fewer than 16 percent of the homeless population are considered "chronically homeless."

---

[246] http://www.endhomelessness.org/pages/snapshot_of_homelessness

- About 10 percent of the homeless population - 62,619 - are veterans.

This translates into approximately 2% of our population being without appropriate housing at any moment of time.

Since we are talking numbers here, let's talk about some other numbers: According to estimates by the Hartford Institute, there are roughly 350,000 religious congregations in the United States of varying size[247] with approximately 63 million individuals in attendance on any given Sunday.[248] If we continue down this math trail we can see there are approximately 100 weekly church-going Bible-believing Christians per homeless person in the United States.

Let's assume $2000 a month would provide food and shelter for one of these homeless individuals. This means that for every 100 church-going American Christians willing to invest $20 per month, a homeless person would not have to be homeless anymore. If we carry this a little further, if all of the 63 million church going Christians in America would donate $20 per month toward food and shelter for the homeless, we could put an end to the homeless problem in America right now. This doesn't seem like something that is beyond our reach or even approaching the ranks of the unthinkable. Homelessness…done!

I realize this is an oversimplification of the issue on many levels and does not take into account those who choose to remain homeless in spite of noble efforts to provide them shelter, but if we could get all of those whose first choice is not

---

[247] http://hirr.hartsem.edu/research/fastfacts/fast_facts.html#numcong
[248] http://hirr.hartsem.edu/research/fastfacts/fast_facts.html#numcong

homelessness off the streets and in suitable shelter, it certainly would be easier to identify and provide appropriate care for those who insist on living outside the bounds of available solutions.

Now lets consider a possible solution that lands a little closer to home and resonates with our relational kingdom values. As an alternative and perhaps better strategy, what if each and every church were to allocate some portion of their facility to one or two apartments that could be made available to someone who is currently homeless. These, our homeless brothers and sisters, would then not only have access to shelter, but be "adopted" into a community of people who care about them rather than warehoused away and apart from the interactional support they likely need.

In exchange for this housing, these individuals could be expected to contribute something in return to the church…whatever was appropriate to the situation. This could include anything from grounds keeping to tech support to stuffing envelopes or whatever, depending on the skill set of the individual. This strategy provides them with a way to contribute something in return for the ability to enjoy safe and decent housing while restoring dignity and self-respect to the individual. It addition, it surrounds them with a community of people who want to see them succeed while providing them with another shot at a productive life they might never have had otherwise.

There is another strategy gaining ground as a possible solution to homelessness, which revolves around structures known as small homes or micro-homes. This type of housing is inexpensive to construct and provides a great alternative to those living without shelter. One group that is taking this strategy a step further is Mobile Loaves & Fishes. MLF is working on a project called Community First! Village, which is a "27 acre master-planned community that will provide affordable, sustainable housing and a supportive community for the disabled, chronically homeless in Central Texas."[249] Here are some of the planned features for this micro-home community:[250]

- An innovative mix of affordable housing options.

- Places for worship, study, and fellowship.

- Memorial garden and columbarium.

- A community garden featuring fruit and nut bearing trees and vegetables.

- A chicken operation, bee hives producing fresh honey and an aquaponics fish operation.

- A workshop with tool bank and art gallery for micro-enterprise opportunities.

- A medical facility for physical and mental health screenings and support services including hospice and respite care.

- Walking trails

- An outdoor theater and Bed & Breakfast for mission visits.

- Walking distance to public transportation

---

[249] http://mlf.org/pave-the-way-home/
[250] http://mlf.org/pave-the-way-home/

- Wi-Fi

This would appear to be a wonderful idea that can hopefully be replicated throughout the country as a way to care for our brothers and sisters who are without suitable shelter.

It is interesting that "contemporary Christians tend to equate morality with sexual ethics, [while] our ancestors defined morality as welcoming the stranger."[251] Taking action to help the homeless "strangers" among us definitely puts us on the road to the "moral" ground we should occupy on this issue.

Marriage

The statistics concerning Christians and marriage are not very good. Let's look at the results from a couple of research studies:

- According to a Barna study released in 2008, being a Christian does not distinguish you from the non-Christian population when it comes to divorce.

Divorce Among Adults Who Have Been Married.[252]

- Evangelical Christians 26%
- Non-Evangelical Christians 33%
- Associated with non-Christian faith 38%
- Atheist or agnostic 30%

---

[251] Bass, *A People's History of Christianity*, 62.
[252] http://www.barna.org/barna-update/article/15-familykids/42-new-marriage-and-divorce-statistics-released

In other research, Bradley Wright, a University of Connecticut sociologist, reviewed an extensive study conducted by the National Opinion Research Center at the University of Chicago and found "Christians, like adherents of other religions, have a divorce rate of about 42%. The rate among religiously unaffiliated Americans is 50%."[253]

While a statistical difference exists in the rates revealed by these two researchers, the overall message remains consistent: being a Christian only gives us a slight edge over non-Christians when it comes to our ability to successfully sustain a marriage. This raises a question: how can we claim to be a people in the world but not of the world when our inability to sustain a successful marriage reflects a fairly worldly standard?

Divorce is a tragedy and yes sometimes it is the best solution, but wouldn't you think if you were to look at a people committed to living out a new kingdom life…a life of a people chosen by God…that something like their divorce rate would be significantly lower than those who are not so chosen? This raises another question: if the divorce rate among Christians were substantially below that of the cultural norms, wouldn't married couples look to Christian marriages as the standard of that which they aspire to attain? If this were possible, how can we get to the place where we could see this happen?

Oftentimes churches make an effort to encourage and enrich the marriages within their community, but these efforts are more than likely linked to a special Marriage Enrichment Weekend held once a year rather than an ongoing

---

[253] http://usatoday30.usatoday.com/news/religion/2011-03-14-divorce-christians_N.htm

commitment by the church to encourage and support activities in which men, women *and* children are provided with opportunities to work together for the common good. Working together towards a common goal binds families together and tends to take the focus off the fulfillment of individual needs and refocus those attentions in the direction of the greater good of the community.

What if rather than segregating community engagement efforts by having the men take on this project, the women take on that project, the teens go on this trip and the children work on that service project … the church instead enabled *family* projects that provided opportunities for the family to work together to help improve the lives of those around them?

In the business world, we would call this *team building* and each year organizations of varying size invest time and money into building better teams in hopes of increasing productivity and subsequently generating greater profits.

> "Teamwork can be very satisfying emotionally for it responds to an ancient desire to participate in something bigger than each of us individually."[254]

Working together as a team "develops the skills of groups of people to look for the larger pictures beyond individual perspectives."[255] In this sense, the psychology of marriage is not that different from the psychology of a team. When the members of either group are focused on higher goals, on goals

---

[254] Peter Koestenbaum, *Leadership: The Inner Side of Greatness*, new and rev. ed., The Jossey-Bass Business and Management Series (San Francisco: Jossey-Bass, 2002), 131.

[255] Peter M. Senge, *The Fifth Discipline: The Art and Practice of the Learning Organization*, rev. and updated. ed. (New York: Doubleday/Currency, 2006), 10.

that allow us to serve the greater needs of those around us, our American individualistic pre-occupation with fulfillment of the self above all else diminishes and ceases to create cracks in the team armor that contribute to splitting the team apart.

What kind of witness would this unity in both marriage and purpose be to those outside the church? One thing we know for sure, we would be witnesses to the truth of Christ that inspires us rather that witness to the scenario in which Christian families are not really that different from families of non-Christians. Once again, as a Church, we can do better.

Earth Care

The topic of Earth Care within Christianity is gaining traction through a growing understanding of what is being called *ecotheology*. In a nutshell, ecotheology focuses on the relationship between religion and ecology;[256] two issues various members of our tribe might be hesitant to connect. However, if all of us would take a moment to get over ourselves, we just might find *theological* correctness aligning with *political* correctness on this particular issue.

The argument for Christian engagement in earth care is really pretty simple. God created the earth and left us to take care of it… essentially until Jesus' return. This is a natural and organic process that involves imitating the actions of God by putting our hands in the dirt and doing a little creating ourselves. This is right and this is natural, but our understanding of God's creation has somehow gone askew as

---

[256] https://www.equinoxpub.com/journals/index.php/JSRNC

we have fallen victim to enlightenment sensibilities of attempting to understand nature using "tools of science rather than theology."[257] This strategy encourages us to maximize life on this earth using the "metrics of market economics rather than the theological virtues of faith, hope, and love."[258]

As those God has chosen to care for creation, one would think the Church would be found at the forefront of issues concerning care for that creation. Unfortunately, instances of this are more the exception than the rule. If we were to attempt to regain some sort of legitimacy in this area, how might we begin to take steps in that direction?

First of all, at bare minimum, we should not be exploiters of God's creation. This earth is not here for us to use and abuse as we choose…seemingly the stance of those who lean more toward a *scorched earth* approach (i.e. Jesus is coming back soon to restore everything so why worry about caring for this our "temporary" home?) This stance, of course, places Christians in the position of users of the earth which lies in direct contrast to one of the primary Biblical characteristics associated with Christianity: that of servant… those who serve the needs of others. We serve the needs of others when we care for them and we serve the needs of others when we care for this our home…our garden…this tiny rock spinning round and round in our little corner of the universe.

Secondly, as Christians we should be the best recyclers of all, especially since we are those who have been recycled…re-

---

[257] Mallory D. McDuff, ed., *Sacred Acts: How Churches Are Working to Protect Earth's Climate* (Gabriola Island, BC: New Society Publishers, 2012), 91.
[258] Ibid.

claimed from death and decay and re-purposed for a new kingdom life.

Where I live, there is a citywide program that picks up recyclables curbside each week. However, this is not universally the case. In those areas where a program such as this is not available, churches have a wonderful opportunity to become the recycling drop off center for their neighborhood. Granted, this would require some degree of effort, but with each item dropped off for recycling, the church would be proclaiming a silent sermon on the responsibilities we all share in caring for God's creation…not to mention a sermon of the importance of redeeming that which is seemingly lost.

In addition, recycling comes with an added value in that recyclables can oftentimes be sold, enabling the project to become an income generator of sorts, or at least a way to minimize the financial outlay necessary to make this recycling effort possible. If becoming a recycling center for your community is not an option, at the very least we should minimize our negative impact through the use of recycled products as much as possible throughout our facilities as well as minimizing conspicuous consumption.

Opportunities for creation care can also be found by those willing to take advantage of the variety of "green" technologies now available to us such as solar power. For example, one church not too far from my home is in the process of installing electric solar panels on their roof. If the idea of creation care is not enough to nudge you in this direction, perhaps a little financial incentive might help as this particular congregation expects to cut their electric bill by 25%, enabling them to save $100,000 dollars over the 30 year life span of the panels.[259]

This savings will provide the church with $100,000 worth of opportunities to re-direct those funds toward more kingdom related activities.

Now, if we were to implement these efforts in churches all across the country just think how much money could be reclaimed from operating expenses and redirected toward more missional efforts of the church.

> "For churches, there is no better opportunity than energy conservation to promote organizational growth, public witness and financial gain at the same time."[260]

All this being said, creation care is an area in which the church has many opportunities to lead by example while making powerful theological statements at the same time.

Politics of Subversion

While our adaptive behaviors in the political arena have done very little to further the cause of Christ, we should not abandon political initiatives but instead engage in what could be called a more subversive form of politics more true to the politics of Jesus.

> "Jesus didn't choose the primacy of the powers of religion/politics or the powers of the individual; He chose a third way - His indwelling presence experienced and displayed through a community of followers who

---

[259] http://www.tulsaworld.com/news/religion/church-has-solar-panels-installed-to-cut-costs-further-environmental/article_3af15afa-ae8b-5e82-942c-d32cfeffe3e3.html

[260] McDuff, *Sacred Acts*, 32.

embody the kingdom of God in their corporate life together."[261]

To better understand this more subversive form of politics, consider the example of Mother Theresa, who rather than fight the caste system of India, chose instead to live in a new kingdom reality in which the caste system did not exist. She could have chosen to organize protests or form political action committees in an effort to nudge the country toward a more equitable political system. But instead, she chose to live within the reality of the new kingdom, where caste is a thing of the past and those viewed by the culture as human debris are set free.

> "This act of living the not-yet state of equality as if it already existed in the now is the truly political act, an act that directly confronts unjust systems by ignoring them and living into a different reality."[262]

Living into a different reality…a kingdom reality…more faithfully aligns with the politics of Jesus and as such provides a much stronger witness to the world over and above our attempts to use politics to enforce our beliefs upon a hesitant culture.

A Punch in the Gut

As part of my doctoral program, we were required to select and attend a conference each year that related to our area of

---

[261] Leonard I. Sweet and Frank Viola, *Jesus Manifesto: Restoring the Supremacy and Sovereignty of Jesus Christ* (Nashville, Tenn.: Thomas Nelson, 2010), 119.
[262] Rollins, *Insurrection*, 150.

study. I chose the Ideation conference founded by Charles Lee.[263] Ideation sounded intriguing and a little different than the standard conference:

> *The Ideation Conference is a unique conference experience that gathers some of the most innovative thinkers and practitioners in the field of social good (e.g., businesses, organizations, influencers, etc.) in order to help fellow practitioners develop thoughts and tangible next steps for greater impact in their respective work.*[264]

The thinkers and practitioners gathering for this event seemed to collectively fit under the umbrella of what we could typically call "social justice" issues. They included: Ben Keesey | CEO of Invisible Children, Chris Heuertz | International Executive Director of Word Made Flesh, Jeff Shinabarger | Founder of Plywood People, Jennifer Vides | Development Director of the Boys & Girls Club of Santa Monica, Joshua Dubois | Special Assistant to President Obama & Executive Director of the White House Office of Faith-Based and Neighborhood Partnerships, Mark Horvath | Founder of InvisiblePeople.tv, Rod Arnold | COO of charity: water, and Sean Carasso | Founder of Falling Whistles among others. The thing that I found interesting about this group was how many of the speakers and attendees were Christians but had chosen to engage in what was obviously hands-on ministry apart from the organized Church.

One of the speakers, a guy named Mark Horvath, spoke to the problem of homelessness in America. He spoke with a

---

[263] Charles Lee is also the author of a good book on how to bring your dreams and passions to life called Good Idea, Now What from Wiley Publishing.
[264] http://www.ideationconference.com

certain authority in that Mark had survived a period of homelessness himself prior to founding InvisiblePeople.tv. Since the conference was in Long Beach California, prior to his presentation Mark did a little research on homelessness in the area and found out there were four times as many churches in the Long Beach area as there were homeless people. Upon revealing this fact he rather emotionally and emphatically stated we needed to "stop evangelizing homeless people... they already know Jesus... instead we need to start being the answer to their prayer." The truth of his statement hit me hard, as I hope it does you.

The solutions to the abundance of needs threatening to overwhelm the capacities of our nation's social welfare system are not political solutions that demand more laws or better laws or more governmental programs or more governmental oversight: the solutions instead are found in a radical and subversive form of politics more true to the politics of Jesus: a group of Jesus' followers living a new kingdom reality into existence. This is a reality in which those who are sick are healed, those who are alone find family, those who are hungry are fed, those who are without appropriate shelter find a home, those in relationships are encouraged, and those who live on this earth become the caretakers of this planet...our home.

When the Church aligns itself with this more Christo-centric form of engagement with the world, this is where we will find Jesus and this is where we will begin to see the first glimpses of the new kingdom Jesus announced and proclaimed.

An Abundance of Opportunity

It has not been my purpose here to address each and every opportunity the church has to show the love of Jesus through a more hands-on living out of the *way*. There is not enough space to consider all the possible areas of engagement we did not address such as race relations, women's rights, individuals with disabilities, our LGBT brothers and sisters, immigrant care, or equal educational opportunities, etc. All of the individuals and families impacted by these and any number of other issues to which God gives you particular insight are worthy of the caring presence only a people of the *way* can provide. To this end, search your heart and pray, but ultimately acknowledge and accept your longing to be in the presence of Jesus can best be fulfilled by locating yourself alongside the people of the margins, because that is always where Jesus can be found.

Part 5 - Big Buts

Chapter 8 - Is Your Big But the Problem?

Diagnostic Strategy: Uncovering Challenges to Rehabilitation

Knowing the reality of our current situation, as well as what we should do about it places us well on the road to rehabilitation for our church...right? Well, not exactly. Connecting these two oftentimes proves problematic as a variety of factors contribute to success or failure in this area. For an example of how this plays out in real life scenarios, let's re-visit our patient examples.

In our patient investigations, we discussed the options available to those with hearing loss, obesity, dizziness, failing memory, and pain that make possible their rehabilitation. Unfortunately, the presence of these options and opportunities in no way guarantees the patient will embrace and accept them as a way to move toward a better life.

• Patients with hearing loss can decide to keep the world at a distance rather than take advantage of the variety of hearing technologies available to them.

• Individuals who know their obesity is causing a decline in their overall health and well-being can choose to take their chances rather than make the necessary modifications to their lifestyle.

• Patients that suffer from dizziness can choose to withdraw from engagement with the activities they used to enjoy rather than participate in therapies to help them regain their balance.

- Those whose memories are slipping away can choose to retreat to the safety of isolation rather than take advantage of the medications and therapies that could help them.

- And those in constant pain can decide to medicate their pain away rather than attempt to address its underlying cause.

We know this to be true, because our own stories are not so different from those of our patients in that our best intentions oftentimes give way to the safety of the well-worn path.

We know, but we do not do.

We learn, but we fail to put into practice.

We feel guilty, but not guilty enough to take action.

And therein we come face to face with the problem.

The problem lies in our *buts*...but not likely the *buts* that first come to mind.

Taking a Look at Our Buts

First, let's clarify what I mean when talking about our "buts." Our *buts* are those things that stand between us and opportunity. For example, consider the following scenarios:

- Hey, do you want to come over for dinner tonight?

    I would *but*…

- We are going to go downtown to do some repairs on this guy's house, why don't you come?

    I would *but*…

- Why don't we go next door and meet the new neighbors?

    I would *but*…

- Hey, what do you think about teaching a class at church?

    I would *but*…

Etc. Etc. Etc.

Buts reveal our doubts.

Buts reveal our insecurities.

Buts reveal our character.

And unfortunately, *buts* reveal the true nature of our beliefs.

This paradoxical position of knowing what to do *but* not doing it is nothing new. Paul was quite forthcoming on this issue as he wrote about his experience:

> *"What I don't understand about myself is that I decide one way,* **but** *then I act another, doing things I absolutely despise."*[265]

Sound familiar? We know what we should do *but* we are hard pressed to do it...our *buts* get in the way...both figuratively and literally. Paul knew what to do and yet his *buts* were a problem, and like Paul, we too know what we should do. However, our *buts* seem to get the best of us.

As a way to better understand our *buts*, let's remain true to our diagnostic model by doing a little research into some big *but* stories in the Bible. These stories can be divided into 3 distinct categories: stories of **disobedience**, stories of **obedience**, and stories of **reluctance**.

Disobedience Stories

Adam & Eve

In the beginning there was God, and God had a plan for creation. God's plan interestingly included a *but*:

> *"And the Lord God commanded the man, 'You may freely eat of every tree of the garden;* **but** *of the tree of the knowledge of good and evil you shall not eat, for in the day that you eat of it you shall die.'"*[266]

---

[265] Romans 7:15 (MSG) emphasis added
[266] Genesis 2:16-17. (emphasis added)

But, we know what happened:

> *"Now the serpent was more crafty than any other wild animal that the Lord God had made. He said to the woman, 'Did God say, 'You shall not eat from any tree in the garden'?' The woman said to the serpent, 'We may eat of the fruit of the trees in the garden;* **but** *God said, 'You shall not eat of the fruit of the tree that is in the middle of the garden, nor shall you touch it, or you shall die.''* **But** *the serpent said to the woman, 'You will not die; for God knows that when you eat of it your eyes will be opened, and you will be like God, knowing good and evil.' So when the woman saw that the tree was good for food, and that it was a delight to the eyes, and that the tree was to be desired to make one wise, she took of its fruit and ate; and she also gave some to her husband, who was with her, and he ate."*[267]

God's instructions were pretty clear. However, temptation came in the form of a *but*…a *but* that caused Eve to question God…to think maybe there were other options to be considered here…to think what she wanted might be better than what God wanted for her. It is not like Eve did not understand the rules. The rules were simple and quite clear. *"Don't eat from the tree of the knowledge of good and evil."* *But,* Eve and subsequently Adam proceeded to do just that. And so it began. Humanity's big *but* entered the picture, and as a result these big *buts* have been causing trouble throughout history.

Abraham

Even though Paul referred to the faith of Abraham in Romans 4 as an example for us all, this man of faith struggled with his own *buts*:

---

[267] Genesis 3:1-6. (emphasis added)

God told Abram (later Abraham) *"'Look toward heaven and count the stars, if you are able to count them.' Then he said to him, 'So shall your descendants be.' And he believed the Lord; and the Lord reckoned it to him as righteousness."*[268]

Initially, Abraham put his faith in this promise as he and Sarai (later Sarah) awaited the arrival of their first child. *But* as time passed and the hope of the promise began to fade, Sarai enlisted her Egyptian servant girl to serve as a surrogate so Abram might have his promised son[269]...a decision that continues to impact our world today. Later, Sarah and Abraham were once again reminded of God's promise of an heir for Abraham through Sarah.[270] This news caused Sarah to laugh out loud since she and Abraham were now well past childbearing age.[271] However, in spite of their disbelief, Abraham and Sarah were blessed with the reality of God's promise: Isaac.[272]

Later in the story in what seems like a cruel and ironic twist, God asks Abraham to do the seemingly unthinkable.

> *"After these things God tested Abraham. He said to him, 'Abraham!' And he said, 'Here I am.' He said, 'Take your son, your only son Isaac, whom you love, and go to the land of Moriah, and offer him there as a burnt offering on one of the mountains that I shall show you.'"*[273]

---

[268] Genesis 15:5-6.
[269] Genesis 16.
[270] Genesis 18:10.
[271] Genesis 18:12
[272] Genesis 21.
[273] Genesis 22:1-2.

It is not hard to imagine the *buts* racing through Abraham's mind at this news...all the ways in which he might try to negotiate some sort of more acceptable compromise. However, the text does not reveal any attempts by Abraham to negotiate on Isaac's behalf.

Perhaps at this later stage of life, Abraham had learned to trust God...to put more faith in the callings of God over and above Abraham's *buts*. *But*, God intervened in this story and provided an alternate sacrifice for Abraham allowing Isaac to live and the prophecy of Genesis 15 to be fulfilled.

Lot & His Wife

At a time when great evil was rampant in the cities of Sodom and Gomorrah, God decided to destroy both of them.[274] The angels who had been sent to accomplish this task warned Lot that he and his family must leave the city to avoid destruction as well:

"Flee for your life; do not look back or stop anywhere in the Plain; flee to the hills, or else you will be consumed."[275]

All was well for Lot and his family until a big *but* got in the way:

***"But** Lot's wife, behind him, looked back, and she became a pillar of salt."*[276]

Even though Lot and his family were well on their way to safety, the temptation of a *but* got in the way and Lot's wife suffered the consequence of her disobedience.

---

[274] Genesis 19.
[275] Genesis 19:17.
[276] Genesis 19:26. (emphasis added)

Stories of Obedience

Now let's turn from stories in which people's *buts* got in the way, to the stories of those who were able to overcome their *buts* and willingly followed God's call on their lives, oftentimes in spite of great opposition.

Noah

God was disappointed in creation. People were not living in the way in which God had hoped they would live, and in what some might consider a rather drastic reaction to the circumstances, God made a decision:

> *"I will blot out from the earth the human beings I have created—people together with animals and creeping things and birds of the air, for I am sorry that I have made them."*[277]

And then, as usual, here comes a big *but*... however, it is a *but* of a different kind.

> ***But** Noah found favor in the sight of the Lord."*[278]

The story tells us that *"Noah was a righteous man, blameless in his generation; Noah walked with God."*[279] While we don't know the details of exactly what being righteous and blameless means in this story, we can infer Noah was someone God could trust...trust enough with the future of creation, for God then gave Noah very specific instructions on how to accomplish God's mission through the building of an ark:

---

[277] Genesis 6:7.
[278] Genesis 6:8. (emphasis added)
[279] Genesis 6:9.

God told Noah, *"For my part, I am going to bring a flood of waters on the earth, to destroy from under heaven all flesh in which is the breath of life; everything that is on the earth shall die."*[280] The Lord then says *"**But** I will establish my covenant with you; and you shall come into the ark, you, your sons, your wife, and your sons' wives with you."*[281] Noah and his family's survival were provided for in God's big *but*.

Noah went on to build the ark while likely becoming the laughing stock of the community. However, whatever personal *buts* Noah may have experienced, they were not enough to prevent him from completing the task of preparing creation for the re-creation that was to come.

Joseph

The story of Joseph is a story full of *buts*. We will only cover a few here for the sake of brevity. Joseph was the son of Isaac and Rebekah and the grandson of Abraham and Sarah. We are told that Isaac loved Joseph more than any of his other sons;[282] as we can imagine, this caused problems with his siblings. Therein we encounter the first *but* of the story.

> *"But when his [Joseph's] brothers saw that their father loved him more than all his brothers, they hated him, and could not speak peaceably to him."*[283]

Because of this, they considered killing Joseph but instead ended up selling him into slavery.[284] *But* God had other plans for Joseph. Joseph's slavery placed him in service to Potiphar,

---

[280] Genesis 6:17.
[281] Genesis 6:18. (emphasis added)
[282] Genesis 37:3.
[283] Genesis 37:4.
[284] Genesis 37:28.

the captain of Pharaohs' guards, which unfortunately also put him in position of becoming the object of Potiphar's wife's desires.[285] *But* Joseph refused her advances and as a result found himself in prison:[286]

> *"But the Lord was with Joseph and showed him steadfast love; he gave him favor in the sight of the chief jailer."*[287]

Later in the story, Pharaoh had a dream no one in his inner court could explain. Joseph was called before Pharaoh to interpret the dream."[288] After doing so, Pharaoh appointed Joseph to be over his entire house, making him second only to Pharaoh in all of Egypt.[289] This placed Joseph in a position to save both Egypt and his extended family from the drought that crippled the area, enabling both to survive and prosper in the years to come.

Joseph had many an opportunities to become bitter in his life, to abandon his faith in God, and to sink into a life of despair and disappointment. *But* instead, Joseph continued to follow the call of God in situations that would oftentimes seem to indicate God was nowhere to be found.

Stories of Reluctance

Next let's look at a couple of stories in the Bible in which those chosen by God for a special assignment were reluctant to

---

[285] Genesis 39:12.
[286] Genesis 39:20.
[287] Genesis 39:21.
[288] Genesis 41:14.
[289] Genesis 41:40.

accept God's call although eventually overcame their reluctance to fulfill God's purposes for their lives.

Jonah

In the story of Jonah, we find one who was at first disobedient, seeking to avoid or run from Gods calling to *"Go at once to Nineveh, that great city, and cry out against it; for their wickedness has come up before me."*[290]

Jonah's big *but* gets him into trouble:

> *"But Jonah set out to flee to Tarshish from the presence of the Lord. He went down to Joppa and found a ship going to Tarshish; so he paid his fare and went on board, to go with them to Tarshish, away from the presence of the Lord."*[291]

And then God's *but* got in the way.

> *"But the Lord hurled a great wind upon the sea, and such a mighty storm came upon the sea that the ship threatened to break up."*[292]

Jonah knew what was causing this great storm; his disobedience. So, he gave the crew of the ship the following instruction:

> *"Pick me up and throw me into the sea; then the sea will quiet down for you; for I know it is because of me that this great storm has come upon you."*[293]

---

[290] Jonah 1:2.
[291] Jonah 1:3.
[292] Jonah 1:4.
[293] Jonah 1:12.

The crew of the ship, with some amount of protest, ended up granting Jonah's request. *But* God did not allow Jonah to perish in the sea. God still had plans for Jonah:

> *"But the Lord provided a large fish to swallow up Jonah; and Jonah was in the belly of the fish three days and three nights."*[294]

At the point of Jonah's submission to the plans of God, God caused Jonah do be saved and delivered onto dry land. Jonah now responded in obedience to God's calling and the people of Nineveh received Jonah's warning to repent in an effort to save them from the judgment of God.

Jonah was at first disobedient, *but* God was able to convince him that obeying the calling of God might be a more favorable response. In the end, God's *but* trumped Jonah's.

Moses

Moses had gone into hiding after killing an Egyptian. While in hiding, Moses married, had children and became a sheepherder. One day while tending the sheep Moses' attention was drawn toward a bush that was engulfed in flames *but* was not being consumed by those flames. Moses' curiosity drew him toward this mysterious flaming bush and it was at this point Moses heard the following words:

> *"'I am the God of your father, the God of Abraham, the God of Isaac, and the God of Jacob.' And Moses hid his face, for he was afraid to look at God."*[295]

---

[294] Jonah 1:17.
[295] Exodus 3:6.

During the course of the conversation Moses also heard the following:

> "*I will send you to Pharaoh to bring my people, the Israelites, out of Egypt.*"[296]

It was here that Moses begins to reveal his *buts*.

> "**But** *Moses said to God, 'Who am I that I should go to Pharaoh, and bring the Israelites out of Egypt?'*"[297]

This was only the first of Moses' *buts* as he proceeded to make numerous attempts to argue with God:

> "*But Moses said to God, 'If I come to the Israelites and say to them, 'The God of your ancestors has sent me to you,' and they ask me, 'What is his name?' what shall I say to them?'*"[298]

Or…

> "*But suppose they do not believe me or listen to me, but say, 'The Lord did not appear to you.'*"[299]

And then Moses responded in a way many of us respond when confronted with a call we are hesitant to accept:

> "*But he said, 'O my Lord, please send someone else.'*"[300]

But, God did not send someone else. God had chosen Moses, and eventually Moses does lead his people out of captivity in Egypt toward their promised land. This story does not turn out so well for Pharaoh however, for his seemingly endless string of

---

[296] Exodus 3:10.
[297] Exodus 3:11. (emphasis added)
[298] Exodus 3:13.
[299] Exodus 4:11.
[300] Exodus 4:13.

buts in defiance of God's demands led to the death of his first born and the destruction of his army. The *buts* we place between God and ourselves come with a cost.

But it's Part of the Plan

The Hebrew Bible contains a variety of stories in which we find a common theme: "the people of Israel do evil, God is angry, he gives them over to [an oppressor], they cry for help, and he sends them a deliverer."[301] The events associated with the calling of these deliverers occur in such a predictable sequence and with such regularity that scholars have given the process a name; they call it *the prophetic call narrative*.

This narrative consists of 6 elements:[302]

1) A theophany (the appearance of God).

2) An introductory word.

3) God's call of the prophet to perform some task.

4) Objection and resistance to the call from the prophet.

5) God's response to the objection, repeating the call and reassuring the prophet.

6) A confirming sign that is foretold.

---

[301] Kenneth Lewis, *Literary Interpretations of Biblical Narratives*, [Nashville: Abingdon Press, 1974],152.

[302] Frank S. Frick, *A Journey through the Hebrew Scriptures*, 2nd ed. (Belmont, CA: Wadsworth/Thomson Learning, 2003), 197-198.

To understand this more clearly, let's begin by taking a look at the story of Gideon through the lens of the prophetic call narrative.

1) A theophany (the appearance of God) - Judges 6:1
    "Now the angel of the LORD came and sat under the oak at Ophrah, which belonged to Joash the Abiezrite, as his son Gideon was beating out wheat in the wine press, to hide it from the Midianites."[303]

Step one: the initial appearance of God before the chosen deliverer. In this instance, we also find a bit of semiotic connective tissue for the location of the appearance echoes that of another divine manifestation:

"Abram passed through the land to the place at Shechem, to the oak of Moreh. At that time the Canaanites were in the land. Then the "LORD appeared to Abram, and said, 'To your offspring I will give this land.'"[304]

It's easy for us to read the stories and overlook these little connections, but when we do so we are not drinking in the full meaning of the text because (as we will remember) everything is there for a reason...every word has meaning. So when the text specifies God independently meeting Gideon and Abram at oak trees, that similarity is not accidental. It is one more piece of the puzzle that contributes to our understanding and in this case connects Gideon with Abram.

The text also mentions Gideon hiding in a wine press to thresh wheat. Threshing wheat in a wine press is unusual

---

[303] Judges 6:11.
[304] Genesis 12:6-7. (NRSV)

because "under normal circumstances, wheat would be threshed on a windy hilltop"[305] where the wind could have its part in the process. Typically we take this to suggest not only the degree to which the Midianites exerted control over the area, but also how fearful Gideon was of these occupiers. However, when viewed from a different perspective, Gideon's ability to continue to provide for his family in the midst of an occupying force suggests Gideon was resourceful or perhaps clever...an attribute that might prove helpful to the call Gideon was about to receive. In any event, locating Gideon in the wine press underscores how once again Israel was under the control of an oppressor and in need of a deliverer.

2) An introductory word - Judges 6:12-13

"The angel of the LORD appeared to him and said to him, 'The LORD is with you, you mighty warrior.' Gideon answers him, 'But sir, if the LORD is with us, why then has all this happened to us? And where are all his wonderful deeds that our ancestors recounted to us, saying, 'Did not the LORD bring us up from Egypt?'" But now the LORD has cast us off, and given us into the hand of Midian."[306]

In this section of the text we not only have step two in the progression of the prophetic call narrative but we also have the interesting juxtaposition of the angel of the LORD calling a man hiding in the wine press a "mighty warrior." From what we know about the story thus far, it is easy to see Gideon as anything but a mighty warrior. And yet ironically, the name Gideon means "Hacker/Chopper."[307]

---

[305] Harold W. Attridge, ed., *The Harpercollins Study Bible: New Revised Standard Version, Including the Apocryphaldeuterocanonical Books with Concordance*, fully rev. and updated. ed. (New York, NY: HarperCollins, ©2006), 356.
[306] Judges 6:12-13.
[307] A. Grame Auld. *"Hacking at the Heart of the Old Testament"* [Vestus Testamentum 39

In ancient times, the meaning of a name was part of a person's identity. Remember Sarah laughing when hearing the news of her impending pregnancy? This resulted in her son being named Isaac; Isaac means laughter.[308] So, the fact that the angel of the LORD first called Gideon by name and then identified him as a "mighty warrior" could indicate a calling forth of the true identity of Gideon as compared to his current circumstance or perhaps how Gideon saw himself as we shall see later.

In the above text, Gideon also challenges the angel with a reminder of Israel's current situation suggesting this reality seems to indicate the apparent absence of God in contrast to the statement *'The LORD is with you.'*[309] The story then proceeds to once again make a connection between Gideon and another primary figure in the story of Israel by mentioning the exodus of God's people from Egypt under the guidance of Moses. Remember, everything in the story is there for a reason.

3) God's call of the prophet to perform some task - Judges 6:14

"Then the LORD turned to him and said, 'Go in this might of yours and deliver Israel from the hand of Midian; I hereby commission you.'"[310]

In this text, we not only continue on in the sequence of the prophetic call narrative, but we also experience a transition. Earlier in the story, the one confronting Gideon was identified as an *"angel of the LORD."* Now, the angel has become "transparent to the LORD himself".[311] This verse indicates the LORD has now taken over the conversation, which adds

---

no. 3 (1989)], 264.
[308] Attridge, *The Harpercollins Study Bible*, 32.
[309] Judges 6:12.
[310] Judges 6:14.
[311] Attridge, *The HarperCollins Study Bible*, 356.

greater emphasis to Gideon's calling for it now comes directly from God. Also, Gideon is told to *"Go in this might of yours,"* perhaps referring back to the initial greeting of *"mighty warrior"*… underscoring the true identity of the man hiding in the wine press.

4) Objection and resistance to the call from the prophet - Judges 6:15

> *"He responded, 'But sir, how can I deliver Israel? My clan is the weakest in Manasseh, and I am the least in my family.'"*[312]

Reluctance to accept the call of God is one of the primary elements of the *prophetic call narrative*. It serves as a way to validate the individual and their calling as authentic by identifying them as one who accepts their calling out of obedience to God rather than someone whose actions are inspired by ambition or selfish motivations. God seems to prefer these reluctant ones.

5) God's response to the objection, repeating the call and reassuring the prophet - Judges 6:16

> *"The LORD said to him, 'But I will be with you, and you shall strike down the Midianites, everyone of them.'"*[313]

This is where God's *but* comes into play as God attempts to reassure Gideon with the promise of God's presence…a presence that will enable Gideon to grow into that which God is calling him to become. At this point let us consider a certain bit of irony within the story that we might otherwise overlook: the man who saw himself as the weakest member of the weakest tribe, who was hiding in the wine press threshing his wheat in fear of the Midianites is now somehow able to muster

---

[312] Judges 6:15.
[313] Judges 6:16.

up the courage to challenge and argue with God; the all-powerful creator of the universe. This sounds more like a mighty warrior than the weakest member of the weakest tribe. In this, we can see God bringing forth in Gideon that which lies in contrast to Gideon's image of himself...a calling forth of Gideon's true identity...that of a mighty warrior and deliverer of God's people.

6) A confirming sign that is foretold - Judges 6:17-19, 19-21, 23-24

Gideon, still reluctant to accept his new identity as deliverer, asks God for a sign:

> *"Then he said to him, 'If now I have found favor with you, then show me a sign that it is you who speak with me.'"*[314]

Gideon then goes into his house, prepares his offering, and returns:[315]

> *"The angel of God said to him, 'Take the meat and the unleavened cakes, and put them on this rock, and pour out the broth,' And he did so. Then the angel of the LORD reached out the tip of the staff that was in his hand, and touched the meat and the unleavened cakes; and fire sprang up from the rock and consumed the meat and the unleavened cakes; and the angel of the LORD vanished from his sight."*[316]

Gideon's story now takes an interesting turn:

> *"Then Gideon perceived that it was the angel of the LORD; and Gideon said, 'Help me, LORD God! For I have seen the angel of the LORD face to face.'"*[317]

---

[314] Judges 6:17.
[315] Judges 6:18-19.
[316] Judges 6:20-21.
[317] Judges 6:22.

Here we see the once reluctant and defiant Gideon become humble and fearful as he no doubt recalls the stories of those who came face to face with God: *"You cannot see my face; for no one shall see me and live."*[318] The fact that Gideon is still alive at this point in the story directly connects Gideon to other rescuers in the Bible who have had such face-to-face encounters and survived:

- *"The LORD used to speak to Moses face to face, as one speaks to a friend."*[319] Moses
- *"For I have seen God face to face, and yet my life is preserved."*[320] Jacob

In spite of these rather dramatic events, Gideon once again asks God for confirmation that he will be victorious in this venture (and then asks for a confirmation of his confirmation!)

"Then Gideon said to God, "In order to see whether you will deliver Israel by my hand, as you have said, I am going to lay a fleece of wool on the threshing floor; if there is dew on the fleece alone, and it is dry on all the ground, then I shall know that you will deliver Israel by my hand, as you have said." And it was so. When he rose early next morning and squeezed the fleece, he wrung enough dew from the fleece to fill a bowl with water. Then Gideon said to God, "Do not let your anger burn against me, let me speak one more time; let me, please, make trial with the fleece just once more; let it be dry only on the fleece, and on all the ground let there be dew." And God did so that night. It was dry on the fleece only, and on all the ground there was dew."[321]

Even though Gideon is the poster child of self-doubt, he does ultimately overcome his buts and accept God's call to defeat

---

[318] Exodus 33:20. (NRSV)
[319] Exodus 33:11.
[320] Genesis 32:30.
[321] Judges 6:37-40.

the Midianites. However, he does so in a manner no one would have seen coming. If you are not familiar with the outcome, you can find the rest of the story in Judges 7.

Other Prophetic Call Narrative Stories

Now let's compare the elements of Gideon's story with several other prophetic call narratives...those of Moses, Isaiah, Jeremiah, and Jonah. The chart below identifies how the verses of each of these stories align with the prophetic call narrative.

	Exodus 3:1-23 Moses	Judges 6:11-24 Gideon	Isaiah 6:1-13 Isaiah	Jeremiah 1:4-10 Jeremiah	Jonah 1-3 Jonah
God's Appearance	Verses 1-3	Verses 11-12	Verses 1-7		
God's Initial Conversation / Contact	Verses 4-6	Verses 12-13	Verse 8		
God's Call	Verses 7-10	Verse 14	Verses 9-13	Verses 4, 5 & 10	Verses 1-2
Objection or Resistance	Verse 11	Verse 15	Verse 5	Verse 6	Verse 3
God's Response or Reassurance	Verse 12-18	Verse 16	Verse 6-7	Verse 7-8	Verse 1:17 & 2:10
God's Sign of Confirmation	Verses 19-22	Verses 17-24		Verse 9	Verses 3:4-5

God's Call

While each story does not contain all six of the elements of our narrative, each story does follow a common trajectory. Let's begin our comparison at the point of God's call:

Moses - *"deliver them from the Egyptians"*[322]

Gideon - *"deliver Israel from the hand of Midian"*[323]

---

[322] Exodus 3:7.
[323] Judges 6:14.

Isaiah - *"go and say to the people"*[324]

Jeremiah - *"I appointed you a prophet to the nations"*[325]

Jonah - *"Go to the great city of Nineveh and preach against it, because of its wickedness."*[326]

Objection or Resistance

In response to their assignment, each of our characters indicates some degree of reluctance (a but) to the task, reminding God of their lack of capability (or in Jonah's case, running away from the assignment and then spending three days in the belly of a whale while he thought things over):

Moses - *"Who am I that I should go to Pharaoh, and bring the Israelites out of Egypt?"*[327]

Gideon - *"But sir, how can I deliver Israel? My clan is the weakest in Manasseh, and I am the least in my family."*[328]

Isaiah - *"Woe is me. I am lost, for I am a man of unclean lips, and I live among a people of unclean lips."*[329]

Jeremiah - *"Ah, LORD God! Truly I do not know how to speak, for I am only a boy."*[330]

Jonah - *"But Jonah ran away from the LORD and headed for Tarshish."*[331]

---

[324] Isaiah 6:9.
[325] Jeremiah 1:5.
[326] Jonah 1:2.
[327] Ex. 3:11.
[328] Judges 6:15.
[329] Isaiah 6:5.
[330] Isaiah 6:6.

God's Response/Reassurance

More often than not, God's assurance that overcomes the buts of the one being called in these stories is manifest in a promise...a promise that God will be with them:

Moses - *"I will be with you."*[332]

Gideon - *"I will be with you."*[333]

Jeremiah - *"I am with you."*[334]

God's response to Isaiah was a little different. Isaiah's concern was that he was not worthy of such a calling due to his *"unclean lips"*[335] and the fact that he lived among *"a people of unclean lips."*[336] In Isaiah's case, God takes action to restore and purify Isaiah with a burning coal stating, *"Now that this has touched your lips, your guilt has departed and your sin is blotted out,"*[337] thus negating Isaiah's objection.

Jonah received his confirmation and assurance when *"the LORD spoke to the fish, and it spewed Jonah out upon the dry land."*[338] Although the story does not directly speak to the moment of Jonah's acceptance of his calling, we do know that when God restated the calling, Jonah immediately departed for Nineveh indicating a certain degree of acceptance on Jonah's part.[339]

---

[331] Jonah 1:3.
[332] Ex. 3:12.
[333] Judges 6:16.
[334] Jeremiah 1:8.
[335] Isaiah 6:5. (NRSV)
[336] Isaiah 6:5. (NRSV)
[337] Isaiah 6:8. (NRSV)
[338] Jonah 2:10. (NRSV)
[339] Jonah 3.

Summary

The first insight we can glean from these stories is that they are told in a particular way to connect the lead character of these stories with others who were chosen by God in Israel's history. Moses, Gideon, Isaiah, Jeremiah, and Jonah each traveled a similar path on their journey from obscurity to one of God's chosen ones.

Secondly, those chosen by God seem to exhibit some degree of reluctance to their assignment. They doubt, they question, and in the case of Gideon, they set up a series of tests so God can reassure them of the truth of their calling. These buts tends to validate their calling and place them in the good company of a long line of reluctant prophets…those chosen by God to fulfill God's purposes.

The third insight addresses what the prophetic call narrative can reveal to each of us as modern day members of the Body of Christ. When we feel God has called us to take on some specific issue or challenge, when we are reluctant or hesitant to think we could actually make a difference in a particular scenario, or feel completely unqualified for the task ahead, we can look to the Biblical prophets for guidance and inspiration for they too felt *unprepared* and *unqualified*. However, when God was *with them*, they were capable of the *unimaginable*.

Interestingly, we see indicators of the prophetic call narrative in the New Testament as well. Let's look at a couple of examples:

Mary's Story

*"In the sixth month the angel Gabriel was sent by God to a town in Galilee called Nazareth, to a virgin engaged to a man whose name was Joseph, of the house of David. The virgin's name was Mary. And he came to her **[1- theophany]** and said, "Greetings, favored one! The Lord is with you." **[2-introductory word]** But she was much perplexed by his words and pondered what sort of greeting this might be. The angel said to her, "Do not be afraid, Mary, for you have found favor with God. And now, you will conceive in your womb and bear a son, and you will name him Jesus. He will be great, and will be called the Son of the Most High, and the Lord God will give to him the throne of his ancestor David. He will reign over the house of Jacob forever, and of his kingdom there will be no end." **[3-God's call of the prophet to perform some task]** Mary said to the angel, "How can this be, since I am a virgin?" **[4-Objection and resistance to the call from the prophet]** The angel said to her, "The Holy Spirit will come upon you, and the power of the Most High will overshadow you; therefore the child to be born will be holy; he will be called Son of God. And now, your relative Elizabeth in her old age has also conceived a son; and this is the sixth month for her who was said to be barren. For nothing will be impossible with God." **[5-God's response to the objection, repeating the call and reassuring the prophet]** Then Mary said, "Here am I, the servant of the Lord; let it be with me according to your word." Then the angel departed from her. In those days Mary set out and went with haste to a Judean town in the hill country, where she entered the house of Zechariah and greeted Elizabeth. When Elizabeth heard Mary's greeting, the child leaped in her womb. And Elizabeth was filled with the Holy*

Spirit and exclaimed with a loud cry, "Blessed are you among women, and blessed is the fruit of your womb. And why has this happened to me, that the mother of my Lord comes to me? For as soon as I heard the sound of your greeting, the child in my womb leaped for joy. And blessed is she who believed that there would be a fulfillment of what was spoken to her by the Lord."[340] ***[6-A confirming sign].***

In Mary's story, we once again see the six criteria in the prophetic call narrative as informing and validating her call to be the mother of Jesus.

Jesus' Story

In the story of Jesus we also find evidence that points the prophetic call narrative.

1) A theophany (the appearance of God)

"And when Jesus had been baptized, just as he came up from the water, suddenly the heavens were opened to him and he saw the Spirit of God descending like a dove and alighting on him."[341]

2) An introductory word

"And a voice from heaven said, "This is my Son, the Beloved, with whom I am well pleased."[342]

3) God's call of the prophet to perform some task

---

[340] Luke 1:26-45.
[341] Matthew 3:16.
[342] Matthew 3:17.

This step in the sequence varies to some degree in that Jesus is not receiving his calling from God but rather announcing his calling. This is unique in the prophetic call narratives but seems appropriate since Jesus is both fully human and fully God. Jesus, as the expression of God on the earth, is capable of speaking for himself:

> *"You say that I am a king. For this I was born, and for this I came into the world, to testify to the truth. Everyone who belongs to the truth listens to my voice."*[343]

> *"I must proclaim the good news of the kingdom of God to the other cities also; for I was sent for this purpose."*[344]

4) Objection and resistance to the call from the prophet

> *"Father, if you are willing, remove this cup from me; yet, not my will but yours be done."*[345]

While this statement is not necessarily an example of objection or resistance, it does show at least a small amount of reluctance to embrace the full consequence of his calling. However, just as Jesus deferred to God in the story of his temptation in the desert, he also defers to God's will here.

5) God's response to the objection, repeating the call and reassuring the prophet

> *"Then an angel from heaven appeared to him and gave him strength."*[346]

6) A confirming sign that is foretold

---

[343] John 18:37.
[344] Luke 4:43.
[345] Luke 22:43.
[346] Luke 22:43.

"Thus it is written, that the Messiah is to suffer and to rise from the dead on the third day, and that repentance and forgiveness of sins is to be proclaimed in his name to all nations, beginning from Jerusalem. You are witnesses of these things."[347]

If the life of Jesus was not enough evidence of his calling, the resurrection surely was. It was predicted and later occurred as confirmation to the truth of Jesus' message, life, and calling. This sign is not so much for Jesus as it is for us.

Our Story

We have observed that callings of God are fairly sequential and follow a predictable pattern which begs the question: Do we, as those who have been chosen by God for participation in the new kingdom life have a prophetic call narrative of our own? Obviously, we cannot dig into the stories of each and every Christian to verify the presence of the prophetic call narrative in their lives. However, we can turn to the Bible to see if we as Christians have indeed been called to a kingdom life in a similar manner. To that end, let us now turn our attention to the process of uncovering a prophetic call narrative we can call our own.

1) A theophany (the appearance of God)

One of the primary tenets of Christianity is that Jesus is one with God. This was an issue the early church struggled with but was eventually codified at the Council of Nicaea when they identified Jesus as *being of one substance with the Father*. This served to affirm that which Jesus himself had said: *"The Father and I are*

---

[347] Luke 24:46-48.

one"[348] or *"Believe me that I am in the Father and the Father is in me."*[349] So, we have a theophany event in that the presence of Jesus was in fact an appearance of God.

2) An introductory word

For those of us who consider ourselves Christians, at some point we were introduced to Christ. This was either through reading the Bible, the works or words of one of the members of the Body of Christ, or through an experience in which the Holy Spirit invaded our space making his presence undeniable. In any event, as Christians we have at some point been introduced to Jesus.

3) God's call of the prophet to perform some task

In the Bible, we have record of Jesus presenting not only his disciples of the day but also us as his future disciples with a mission...a task to perform:

"Go therefore and make disciples of all nations, baptizing them in the name of the Father and of the Son and of the Holy Spirit, and teaching them to obey everything that I have commanded you."[350]

4) Objection and resistance to the call from the prophet

The majority of this book thus far has been a discussion of our reluctance to engage in a way of life that manifests itself in our following in the footsteps of Christ. We each have a different story and a variety of reasons for our reluctance. However, in the end we find our *buts* in alignment with the *buts*

---

[348] John 10:30.
[349] John 14:11.
[350] Matthew 28:19-20.

of those who have gone before us; our *buts* continue to get between ourselves and the callings of God.

5) God's response to the objection, repeating the call and reassuring the prophet

As you will remember, God's reassurance of the prophets in the Hebrew Bible was a promise to be *with them* as they moved forward into God's purposes.

Joseph - *"But the Lord was with Joseph."*[351]

Moses - *"I will be with you."*[352]

Gideon - *"I will be with you."*[353]

Jeremiah - *"I am with you.*[354]

Today we have the same promise from the source of our calling when Jesus said:

"And remember, I am with you always, to the end of the age."[355]

We will discuss this in greater detail later.

6) A confirming sign that is foretold

Jesus, the Messiah, is the sign that has been foretold since the beginning of history.

"Every bit of Scripture is part of the same great story of that one person and that one story's plotline of creation, revelation, redemption, and consummation[356]."

---

[351] Genesis 39:21.
[352] Ex. 3:12.
[353] Judges 6:16.
[354] Jeremiah 1:8.
[355] Matthew 28:19-20.

It is also confirmed in the writings of Luke:

> "Then beginning with Moses and all the prophets, he interpreted to them the things about himself in all the scriptures."[357]

The confirmation to our calling comes in the form of a resurrection, a confirming sign that serves as the authentication of our call.

Making it Personal

And so, we find ourselves called in a manner that echoes the way in which many a prophet has been called throughout history. God appears, God calls, God reassures, and God confirms, and yet we find ourselves reluctant, hesitant, and dangerously close to out and out rebellion against God's intentions for us. Placing our desires ahead of God's plans for us is tempting. It has always been tempting. It is a garden temptation that continues to haunt us. Adam and Eve had a big *but* in the garden and we have our big *buts* as well.

We live in a world where our schedules seem to be maxed out with work, kids, sports, dance classes, and of course our need to designate enough time to keep up with our favorite television shows or watch a movie or two. In our weaker moments, some of us might even reluctantly admit we feel a tug at our hearts to engage in some sort of care for those less fortunate, but we are just not sure what we are called to do…there are so many options and so many questions, and as post-moderns, wrestling with the question somehow seems to

---

[356] Sweet and Viola, *Jesus: a Theography*, x.
[357] Luke 24:27.

be enough. So, we embrace our reluctance while waiting on our burning bush experience before attempting to engage in what we know we are already called to do.

Maybe we are more than reluctant. Maybe we are afraid. Maybe working with *those people* is kind of scary. I mean we see them at the street corner asking for food or cash on our way to the mall. I am not very good at saying no, so they would probably take advantage of me (says the dialog in our heads). Or perhaps in an attempt to assuage our guilt we write a check or make a donation to some philanthropic organization or our church: *we do hire those people to do this kind of work for us don't we?*

Or possibly we still bear the scars from the last time we attempted to make a difference; scars that make us reluctant to jump into the mayhem once again; scars that remind us of the cost that accompanies entering into the suffering of others.

These are just a few of our *buts*...buts that ironically align with the *buts* in our patient examples.

- *Buts* that cause us to turn a deaf ear to Jesus' call to follow him. (hearing loss)

- *Buts* that cause us to rationalize and obscure our current condition. (obesity)

- *Buts* that confine the church to the familiar terrain of our sanctuaries. (dizziness)

- *Buts* that encourage us to forget who we are in Christ. (loss of memory)

- *Buts* that eventually cause us to go numb to those in need. (pain)

They are buts that separate us from one another; buts that encourage us to engage in adaptive behaviors; buts that ultimately keep our relationship with Jesus at arms length rather than enabling us to wrap our arms around the cross we are destined to carry as his followers.

Cross carrying comes with a cost and it is a cost many of us are not willing to pay. Therein lies at least part of our problem. We are attracted toward those things that taste better, go faster, are more comfortable, or make something easier…not those things that are going to end up hurting us or making our lives more difficult. Pain and difficulty are to be avoided…pleasure and simplicity are to be pursued; at least that is the underlying myth of much of Western culture.

As capitalists we are supposed to seek the highest return on our investments. We are supposed to pay the least amount we can for the highest quality we can afford. As such, we are quite willing to use our personal resources to avoid suffering rather than dive headlong into the seemingly endless stream of suffering that threatens to overtake our world. In fact, new products tempt us with their claim to do more for less or make our lives easier…not more difficult.

In light of postmodern self-centeredness, self-sacrifice is a pretty tough sell. Saving money until you can buy a new car or new outfit or new baseball bat or whatever is not how the system works. We want it now and we want it with the least pain possible…even weight loss: just take a pill and you can lose weight and eat whatever you like: at least that is what the infomercial says. We typically prefer life on our own terms. Trying to convince us that we should lean more toward self-sacrifice than self-interest is an uphill battle, and as it turns out, one of our biggest *buts* to overcome.

In this, we are at best *reluctant* and at worst *disobedient* when it comes to our calling to love our neighbors as ourselves when loving ourselves is such a better bargain. Our diagnosis is perhaps better stated in the words of the comic strip Pogo from years ago: *"We have met the enemy and he is us."*

But Who Am I?

In our discussion we have seen how those who have gone before us reacted when God called upon them to do great things… how their *buts* tried to get in the way:

Moses - *"Who am I that I should go to Pharaoh, and bring the Israelites out of Egypt?"*[358]

Gideon - *"But sir, how can I deliver Israel? My clan is the weakest in Manasseh, and I am the least in my family."*[359]

Isaiah - *"Woe is me. I am lost, for I am a man of unclean lips, and I live among a people of unclean lips."*[360]

Jeremiah - *"Ah, LORD God! Truly I do not know how to speak, for I am only a boy."*[361]

Jonah - *"But Jonah ran away from the LORD and headed for Tarshish."*[362]

---

[358] Exodus 3:11.
[359] Judges 6:15.
[360] Isaiah 6:5.
[361] Jeremiah 1:6.
[362] Jonah 1:3.

Just like these icons of the faith, we tend to place our *buts* before God rather than engage in our mission:

But I could never do that…

But I don't have enough time as it is…

But I am not qualified to take on that issue…

But isn't that what the staff at church is supposed to do…

The list goes on and on as our *buts* get the best of us while the savior who died for our sins gets what is left. Our *buts* are large and our *buts* are numerous. Today as in antiquity, some things never seem to change: our big *buts* are a problem…

So, how do we dislodge ourselves for our buts and rise above this state of inaction?

What is the straw that breaks our reluctant *buts*, the thing that causes God's people to return to the *way*, the *way* that truly is the answer to our prayer…*on earth as it is in heaven*?[363]

In our study of the prophetic call narrative, the final element that seemed to tip the scales and cause God's reluctant prophets to do that which they were hesitant to do was a promise…a promise from God…a promise that God would be with them.

Moses - *"I will be with you."*[364]

Gideon - *"I will be with you."*[365]

Jeremiah - *"I am with you."*[366]

---

[363] Matthew 6:10
[364] Exodus 3:12.
[365] Judges 6:16.

Isaiah – *"Do not fear, for I am with you, do not be afraid, for I am your God; I will strengthen you, I will help you, I will uphold you with my victorious right hand."*[367]

We can also add:

Joshua - *"No one shall be able to stand against you all the days of your life. As I was with Moses, so I will be with you; I will not fail you or forsake you."*[368]

Jacob - *"But now thus says the LORD, he who created you, O Jacob, he who formed you, O Israel: Do not fear, for I have redeemed you; I have called you by name, you are mine. When you pass through the waters, I will be with you; and through the rivers, they shall not overwhelm you; when you walk through fire you shall not be burned, and the flame shall not consume you."*[369]

The promise of *God with us* is a garden promise; a promise that brings us back into alignment with God's original intentions; a promise that brings us back into proper relationship with our creator; a relationship that was broken in that garden; a relationship that when absent causes us to doubt, to hesitate, to be reluctant to do those things we have been called to do.

So, as a way to overcome our reluctance to follow God's call on our lives, we need to ask a question:

Do we have the reassurance of *God with us* today?

---

[366] Jeremiah 1:8.
[367] Isaiah 41:10.
[368] Joshua 1:5.
[369] Isaiah 43:1-2.

To help answer this question, let's go to the words of Isaiah for this is where we will find our first hint of an answer.

> *"Therefore the Lord himself will give you a sign. Look, the young woman is with child and shall bear a son, and shall name him Immanuel."*[370]

Years later, when telling the story of the birth of this special one, Matthew refers back to the writings of Isaiah's prophecy:

> *All this took place to fulfill what had been spoken by the Lord through the prophet: "Look, the virgin shall conceive and bear a son, and they shall name him Emmanuel," which means, "God is with us."*[371]

And therein we find our answer: God's assurance throughout history to God's people when calling them to a story beyond their imaginations was that they would not be alone; God would be with them.

In the New Testament, Jesus arrives on the scene as the flesh and blood manifestation of *God with us: Emmanuel*. *God with us* is no longer something we have to be uncertain about. *God with us* is no longer something we have to be reminded of in association with a specific call or specific person or specific action. No. Jesus is *Emmanuel: God with us* as we live our new kingdom lives on this earth.

God with us was that which gave confidence and assurance to God's chosen ones in ages past and *God with us* in Jesus is that which gives us confidence and assurance today. In the words of Jesus: *"I am with you always, to the end of the age."*[372]

---

[370] Isaiah 7:14.
[371] Matthew 1:22-23.

But, before we get all comfortable with our position of post resurrection privilege found in the enduring presence of *God with us,* we should make note that this relational promise comes with a rather large *but* of its own:

> *"Not everyone who says to me, 'Lord, Lord,' will enter the kingdom of heaven, but only the one who does the will of my Father in heaven."*[373]

And there it is: the biggest of the *buts*.

Apparently, our efforts to acknowledge Jesus as Lord (believing properly) are not enough to enter into the kingdom, for according to Jesus we are only credentialed for that in the doing of the will of God.

We are fortunate in that God does not call us to do the impossible even though it may seem improbable and unimaginable at the time, which understandably can contribute to our reluctance. However, rather than allowing this reluctance to distance us from God's call on our lives, it instead serves to locate us in the good company of those God has called in the past for their courage to persevere was inspired by a promise still in effect today…the promise of God with us. This promise was enough for them and it should be enough for us.

- Did Abraham immediately trust God to give him a son?

- Did Joseph understand how all of his trials and tribulations would eventually put him in position to save both Egypt and Israel?

---

[372] Matthew 28:20.
[373] Matthew 7:21.

- Did Jonah upon hearing God's call to go to Nineveh jump right up and head in that direction?

- Did Moses upon seeing the burning bush and hearing the voice of God, immediately accept God's call on him to lead his people to freedom?

- Did Gideon, the least of his kinsmen think God was correct in choosing him to free his people from the Midianites?

No. However, with the assurance of *God with them*, the seemingly *unprepared* and *unqualified* went on to do the *unimaginable*...and so can we.

> "The Bible is not the story of what to expect in life, but the story of what not to expect in life--dead men walking, water turning to wine, missions impossible, etc. The Bible is not the story of 'Great Expectations,' but 'Great Unexpectations."[374]

So, when we live in the land of our great unexpectations, accepting (even if reluctantly) the calling of God to love our neighbors as ourselves, the new kingdom is manifested...God's will is being done...we truly become *those who do the will of the Father.*[375]

"For nothing will be impossible with God."[376]

---

[374] Leonard Sweet, facebook post, April 4, 2013.
[375] Matthew 7:21.
[376] Luke 1:37.

Part 6 - Conclusion

Chapter 9 - Conclusion

Cross Roads

And so we find ourselves at a crossroads. Will we allow the waves of cultural resistance currently splashing in our faces encourage us to seek shelter from the storm in the safety of our sanctuaries, or will we struggle against the current that threatens to pull us under in search of better footing…footing from which we can not only weather the storm, but provide a beacon of hope to a world seemingly awash with reasons to discount the truth of our testimony?

We have all heard faith comes by hearing and as a result have established a multitude of venues in which the Word of God can be heard. However, talk in postmodern culture tends to fall on deaf ears without actions that validate that talk.

> *"Merely hearing God's law is a waste of your time if you don't do what he commands. Doing, not hearing, is what makes the difference with God."*[377]

Yes, beliefs are important for they shape who we are, but our identity is revealed not through our beliefs or our talk, but through our actions.

---

[377] Romans 2:13. (MSG)

Are You the One?

When John the Baptist sent his disciples to ask Jesus if he was the Messiah,[378] what was Jesus' reply?

> *"Go and tell John what you hear and see: the blind receive their sight, the lame walk, the lepers are cleansed, the deaf hear, the dead are raised, and the poor have good news brought to them. And blessed is anyone who takes no offense at me."*[379]

Jesus did not answer John's identity question with a list of 10 reasons why he was the Messiah, nor did he provide a history lesson of who he was or how he came to be. No, Jesus pointed to the evidence of his actions.

- The blind see.
- The lame walk.
- The lepers are cleansed.
- The deaf hear.
- The dead are raised and the poor have good news delivered to them.

The truth of Jesus' identity was found in what he did, not in the beliefs he claimed to embrace. This is a lesson we have forgotten, and a lesson that would serve us well to re-learn as we begin to re-engage our collective Christian calling.

---

[378] Matthew 11:3, Luke 7:19.
[379] Matthew 11:1-6.

Living the Story

Francis Chan tells a story that makes an important point. As the story goes, one day Francis asked his daughter to clean her room. His daughter responded by immediately going to her room, which Francis thought was indicative of his good parenting skills. However, a few days later the topic came up again when she told him she had been thinking about his request that she clean her room. She told him she knew his request was important so she gathered up a group of her friends to investigate it further. They studied the phrase and the variety of meanings the phrase could possibly have, and they could now even recite the phrase in a variety of languages: Greek and Hebrew no less. However, in spite of this flurry of activity to better understand the meaning of what her father had said…her room had not been cleaned.

In many ways, this is how we respond to the commands of Jesus. We gather together. We study. We contemplate alternate meanings and look to original languages to help us better understand. But, we don't actually do what Jesus' asked. We learn about it. We consider it important. But more often than not, they are beliefs we claim to embrace, but beliefs that never make it into the realm of behaviors.

Francis Chan asked his daughter to clean her room because he wanted her to clean her room, not because he wanted her to better understand the meaning of a clean room, and Jesus asks us to love our neighbors as we love ourselves not because he wants us to develop a better understanding of what loving our neighbors means, but because he wants us to love our neighbors.

We are all chapters in an ongoing story, not a people whose purpose is to study the story.

> *The sequel to the New Testament is being written now, by action and suffering. Saintly souls are in the succession of the prophets and the Apostles, not by writing canonical books, but by continuing the history of divine purpose with their lives whose moments are so many syllables and sentences through which it is vividly expressed. The books the Holy Spirit is writing are living, and every soul a volume in which the divine author makes a true revelation of his word, explaining it to every heart, unfolding it in every moment.*[380]

The stories we need to be living are evidence to the truth of Jesus' claims and evidence a world in search of meaning desperately needs to experience.

As Christians, and collectively the Church, we need a more compelling story than the call to a set of beliefs. We need to live a new kingdom story that invites those who find themselves battered and broken on the treacherous shores of self-interest into a community of people whose primary concern is not themselves.

In the interviews David Kinnaman conducted for his book *You Lost Me*, we find a couple of insightful observations concerning what individuals outside the church would like to see in a community of Christians. Their expectations seem to align with our diagnosis.

---

[380] Jean Pierre de Caussade, *Sacrament of the Present Moment*, renovaré ed., trans. Kitty Muggeridge and Richard J. Foster (San Francisco: Harper & Row, 1989, 1982), 74.

I want you to be someone I want to grow up to be like. I want you to step up and live by the Bible's standards. I want you to be inexplicably generous, unbelievably faithful, and radically committed. I want you to be a noticeably better person than my humanist teacher, than my atheist doctor, than my Hindu next-door neighbor. I want you to sell all you have and give it to the poor. I want you to not worry about your health like you're afraid of dying. I want you to live like you actually believe in the God you preach about. I don't want you to be like me; I want you to be like Jesus. That's when I'll start listening.[381] Emma Sleet - student, Lexington, Kentucky

Or…

I have trouble reconciling the disconnect between what the church is saying and what its members are doing. I fail to understand the application when the church tells me to live in accordance with the Bible, but the "scripture" I see its members live by is titled "If I Work Hard I Am Entitled to Whatever Makes Me Happy." I understand the concept of providing for my family, but I'm disappointed when conversations about new granite countertops seem to carry more weight than those about following Christ. I see so much work for financial gain, by both church members and churches themselves, and I don't think that is what I should be pursuing for the sake of Christ.[382] Stewart Ramsey, co-founder of Krochet Kids International

The disdain these two individuals express for the status quo is eloquent and clear: they want to see a people who actually live out what they say they believe, who live in ways that stand

---

[381] David Kinnaman, *You Lost Me: Why Young Christians Are Leaving Church…and Rethinking Faith* (Grand Rapids: Baker Books, 2011), Kindle Locations 4043-4050.
[382] Ibid., Kindle Locations 4052-4056.

counter to the culture rather than embrace the culture, and whose actions better the lives of those around them. In essence, they want to see a group of people living the *truth* in a *way* that leads to *life*.

Postmodernity locates us in a place where a mere presentation of the truth of the Gospel is not enough, for we live in a culture where competing truth claims stand on equal footing. In this climate, the one thing that can tip the cultural scales in favor of Jesus is evidence; the evidence of a people living out those truths and making the world a better place.

As Christians, we are people of the resurrection...those whose lives have been restored through a most subversive Gospel, a Gospel that dares to suggest those of us who find ourselves dead tired and at dead ends, trapped within the tombs of our desperate situations are able to rise up and walk out of those tombs, revived, renewed, and resurrected. The resurrection way is the *way* that provides evidence of the *truth* that leads to a new kingdom *life*.

A Church of Significance

From our discussion of semiotics earlier in the book, we saw how the meaning of words can change for a variety of reasons. In a sense, this is what we are experiencing in Christianity, as our faith and our Church have taken on new meaning: meaning that lies at some distance from its original intentions.

This situation is both enabled and encouraged in that what was once signified by our faith is now less than significant in the lives of those who claim to be Christians.

For our Church to be able to signify something more true to its origins, we are going to have to live in ways that resurrect this meaning in a Church many see as dead to the world. In other words, it's time for us to roll away the stone and walk out of our sanctuaries to "astonish a weary world with the beauty of the Gospel."[383]

> "If the church is operating properly in a given locality, the kingdom of God is seen. Justice, peace, love, mutual care, and giving, are made visible. Christ is seen on the earth again."[384]

In this resurrection witness of Christ's presence alive and active on this earth, we provide the most compelling witness possible… a witness that is not constrained by our *buts*.

A friend of mine recently observed: "Christianity is not a witness protection program."[385] But, in may ways this is exactly what it has become as we gather together in the safety of our sanctuaries, metaphorically circling the wagons to defend against a culture that wants nothing to do with us. However, a proper Christian witness is not that which insulates us from the challenges of living out our faith, but instead is a witness that provides evidence to the truth of our convictions…shining light into the dark places of our world. He then went on to say when we treat Christianity as a witness protection program, "we are guilty of perjury for not providing an accurate testimony."[386] Lest we be found guilty of the verdict postmodern culture has pronounced on us, it is time to be proper witnesses to our faith.

---

[383] Brian Zahnd, *Beauty Will Save the World* (Lake Mary, Fla.: Charisma House, 2012), xvii.
[384] Sweet and Viola, *Jesus: a Theography*, 120.
[385] Thanks to Bryce Ashlin-Mayo for this insight.
[386] Thanks to Bryce Ashlin-Mayo for this insight.

Christian identity is not manifest in the maintenance of proper doctrine or laying claim to a set of beliefs. Our Christian identity is manifest in the living out of those beliefs in ways that point to Jesus, not only as Lord but also as the inspiration of those actions.

> "The core of Christianity is not simply doctrine, vital though that is, but devotion and discipleship in our whole life."[387]

If we truly want to be with Jesus now *and* at the end of the age, then Jesus is not found in the idea of Jesus or in belief in Jesus. Instead, Jesus is found walking alongside those suffering through the miseries of life. And, it is here that Christianity will find itself once again.

A Most Important Question

At the end of my wife's diagnostic investigations when she knows what is wrong with the patient and knows the treatment that will likely enable their rehabilitation, she asks them a question: *Are you ready to get better?* It is a simple question, but the answer is anything but simple; for one answer requires nothing of the patient, while the other answer may take everything they've got.

This question "are you ready to get better?" echoes one Jesus asked a man in need of healing in Jerusalem. In the story, Jesus comes upon a pool where many individuals that are blind, lame, or paralyzed gather in search of healing. They believed when the waters of the pool were stirred, they became

---

[387] James D.G. Dunn and Alan M. Suggate, *The Justice of God: a Fresh Look at the Old Doctrine of Justification by Faith* (Grand Rapids, Mich.: Wm. B. Eerdmans Publishing Company, 1994), 47.

healing waters for those able to maneuver themselves into the pool. Lying near the pool was a man who had been ill for thirty-eight years, unable to make it into the pool for healing. Jesus noticed him and asked that fateful question: *"Do you want to be made well?"*[388]

Interestingly, the man presented Jesus with his *buts*: *"Sir, I have no one to put me into the pool when the water is stirred up; and while I am making my way, someone else steps down ahead of me."*[389] Then Jesus, the promise of *God with us* responded: *"Stand up, take your mat and walk."*[390] The man was immediately healed.

And so, at the end of our diagnostic investigation we have come to see ourselves for what we are: a Church full of *buts*, a Church with a variety of excuses why we can not truly engage in the *way* of Jesus. However, as we find ourselves in the presence of Jesus…Immanuel…God with us, Jesus asks us a question: *"Do you want to be made well?"*[391]

---

[388] John 5:6.
[389] John 5:7.
[390] John 5:8.
[391] John 5:6.

So, Which New Normal Will We Choose?

Will we embrace the New Normal of our present downward trajectory, trying only to keep our Church as comfortable as possible in its final hours?

Or…

Will we pursue a different New Normal…a New Normal that locates us in the presence of Jesus, walking alongside those who have seemingly landed on the wrong side of life's tracks.

One way leads to death.

The other *way* walks in *truth* making possible a kingdom *life*.

I have a decision to make.

You have a decision to make.

We have a decision to make

Our decision will determine the future of our Church.

Afterword

First Steps

Each journey begins with the first steps and for us to begin taking steps in the direction of rehabilitation for our Church we are going to have to start with some conversations. We need to talk about it. We need to pray about it. And then, we need to do something about it.

We already know God is calling the Church to care for our neighbors in need; we just need to dislodge ourselves from our "buts" and get to work.

Don't put it off any longer.

Don't try to save the world, just do your best to save a little part of it. Our world is faced with almost overwhelming challenges. It is easy to let the enormity of those challenges crush us under their weight. However, God so loved the world and we are to love our neighbors.

So pick one…maybe one of these:

- Be the church that helps people get healthy.

- Be the church that cares for the elderly or supports adoption and adoptive parents.

- Be the church that will not let people in your community go hungry.

- Be the church that cares for the homeless.

- Be the church that helps build healthy marriages and relationships.

- Be the church that is leading efforts toward stewardship of God's creation.

But more importantly, be the Church.

Companion Resources

As a way to help you in your efforts to re-engage in the *way* of Jesus, there are several online resources available at www.thomaseingram.com. These resources include a small group discussion guide, a Road Map to Getting Off Our Buts, and links to websites where you can not only share your particular mission opportunity with a wider audience, but also perhaps join together with churches or ministries currently active in the areas of your interest.

Additional Initiatives

Join Leonard Sweet and I at crowdsourcingtheology.com as we research ways in which crowdsourcing can be used to solve some of the more difficult problems facing our Church. We would love your help.

Bibliography

Anderson, Ray S. An Emergent Theology for Emerging Churches. Downers Grove, Ill.: IVP Books, 2006.

Auld, A. Grame. "Hacking at the Heart of the Old Testament." *Vestus Testamentum* 39 no. 3 (1989): 257-267.

Standard Version, Including the Apocryphaldeuterocanonical Books with Concordance. fully rev. and updated. ed. New York, NY: HarperCollins, 2006.

Bass, Diana Butler. *A People's History of Christianity: The Other Side of the Story.* 1 Reprint ed. Philadelphia, Pa.: HarperOne, 2010.

Boring, Eugene. *The New Interpreter's Bible.* Edited by Leander Keck. Vol. 8. Nashville: Abingdon Press, ©1994-2004.

Bromiley, Geoffrey W., *The International Standard Bible Encyclopedia: Vol. 1-4.* Grand Rapids, MI: Eerdmans Pub Co, 1995.

Brooks, James A. "The Kingdom of God in The New Testament." *Southwestern Journal Of Theology* 40, no. 2 (March 1, 1998): 21-37.

Brown, Peter. *Lectures On the History of Religions.* Vol. 13, *The Body and Society: Men, Women, and Sexual Renunciation in Early Christianity.* New York: Columbia University Press, 1988.

Caussade, Jean Pierre de. *Sacrament of the Present Moment.* renovaré ed. Translated by Kitty Muggeridge and Richard J. Foster. San Francisco: Harper & Row, 1989, 1982.

Chandler, Daniel. *Semiotics: the Basics.* 2nd ed. New York: Routledge, 2007.

Dunn, James D.G., and Alan M. Suggate. *The Justice of God: a Fresh Look at the Old Doctrine of Justification by Faith.* Grand Rapids, Mich.: Wm. B. Eerdmans Publishing Company, 1994.

Ernest, James D. *Theological lexicon of the New Testament.* Peabody, MA: Hendrickson Publishers, 1994.

Ferrell, Prof. Lori Anne., *The Bible and the People.* New York: Yale University Press, 2008.

Fitch, David E. *The Great Giveaway: Reclaiming the Mission of the Church from Big Business, Parachurch Organizations, Psychotherapy, Consumer Capitalism, and Other Modern Maladies.* Grand Rapids, MI: Baker Books, 2005.

France, R.T. *The Gospel According to Matthew.* Grand Rapids: Wm. B. Eerdman Publishing Company, 1985.

Frick, Frank. *A Journey Through the Hebrew Scriptures.* Belmot: Thomson Wadsworth, 2003.

Garland, David E. *Reading Matthew: A Literary and Theological Commentary.* Reading the New Testament Series. Macon, Ga.: Smyth & Helwys Pub., ©2001.

Gonzalez, Justo L. *The Story of Christianity, Volume 1: The Early Church to the Dawn of the Reformation (Story of Christianity).* New York: HarperOne, 1984.

Gregory, Brad S. *The Unintended Reformation: How a Religious Revolution Secularized Society.* Cambridge, Mass.: Belknap Press of Harvard University Press, 2012.

Grenz, Stanley J. *A Primer On Postmodernism*. Grand Rapids, Mich.: Wm. B. Eerdmans Publishing Company, 1996.

Hall, Sean. *This Means This, This Means That: A User's Guide to Semiotics*. London: Laurence King Publishers, 2007.

Hart, David Bentley. *The Story of Christianity: An Illustrated History of 2000 Years of the Christian Faith*. London: Quercus Books, 2008.

Hauerwas, Stanley. *A Community of Character: Toward a Constructive Christian Social Ethic*. Notre Dame: University of Notre Dame Press, 1991.

Hunter, James Davison. *Culture Wars: The Struggle to Define America*. New York: BasicBooks, 1991.

Hunter, James Davison. *To Change the World: the Irony, Tragedy, and Possibility of Christianity in the Late Modern World*. New York: Oxford University Press, USA, 2010.

Kaveny, M. Cathleen. "The Order of Widows: What the Early Church Can Teach Us About Older Women and Health Care." *Christian Bioethics: Non-Ecumenical Studies in Medical Morality* 11, no. 1 (2005): 11-34.

Kinnaman, David. *You Lost Me: Why Young Christians Are Leaving Church...and Rethinking Faith*. Grand Rapids: Baker Books, 2011.

Koestenbaum, Peter. *Leadership: The Inner Side of Greatness*. new and rev. ed. The Jossey-Bass Business and Management Series. San Francisco: Jossey-Bass, 2002.

Lewis, Kenneth. *Literary Interpretations of Biblical Narratives*. Nashville: Abingdom Press, 1974.

Lupton, Robert D. *Toxic Charity: How Churches and Charities Hurt Those They Help (and How to Reverse It)*. New York: HarperOne, 2012..

McDuff, Mallory D., ed. *Sacred Acts: How Churches Are Working to Protect Earth's Climate*. Gabriola Island, BC: New Society Publishers, 2012.

Merritt, Jonathan. *A Faith of Our Own: Following Jesus Beyond the Culture Wars*. New York: FaithWords, 2012.

Olson, Roger E. *The Story of Christian Theology: Twenty Centuries of Tradition and Reform*. New York: IVP Academic, 1999.

Pojman, Louis P. *Who Are We?: Theories of Human Nature*. New York: Oxford University Press, USA, 2005.

Rauschenbusch, Walter. *The Righteousness of the Kingdom*. Nashville: Abingdon Press, 1968.

Rollins, Peter. *Insurrection*. Nashville, Tenn.: Howard Books, 2011.

Sakenfield, Katherine. *The New Interpreter's Dictionary of the Bible*. Nashville: Abingdon Press,
2006.

Senge, Peter M. *The Fifth Discipline: The Art and Practice of the Learning Organization*. rev. and updated. ed. New York: Doubleday/Currency, 2006.

Sweet, Leonard. *Nudge: Awakening Each Other to the God Who's Already There*. Colorado Springs, CO: David C. Cook, 2010.

Sweet, Leonard I., and Frank Viola. *Jesus Manifesto: Restoring the Supremacy and Sovereignty of Jesus Christ*. Nashville, Tenn.: Thomas Nelson, 2010.

Sweet, Leonard, and Frank Viola. *Jesus: a Theography*. Nashville, Tenn.: Thomas Nelson, 2012.

Sweet, Leonard I. *Giving Blood: A Fresh Paradigm for Preaching*. Grand Rapids, MI: Zondervan, 2014.

Sweet, Leonard I. *The Well-Played Life: Why Pleasing God Doesn't Have to Be Such Hard Work*. Carol Stream, IL: Tyndale House Publishers, Inc., 2014.

Wright, N. T. *Simply Jesus: Who He Was, What He Did, Why It Matters*. New York: HarperOne, 2011.

Yoder, John Howard. *The Politics of Jesus: Vicit Agnus Noster*. 2nd ed. Grand Rapids, Mich.: Wm. B. Eerdmans Publishing Company, 1994.

Young, Robert. *Young's Analytical Concordance to the Bible*. Peabody: Hendrickson Publishers 01/01/, 2005.

Zahnd, Brian. *Beauty Will Save the World*. Lake Mary, Fla.: Charisma House, 2012.

Bible Sources

All Bible quotations from the New Revised Standard Version Bible (unless otherwise noted), copyright ©1989, Division of Christian Education of the National Council of Churches of Christ in the U.S.A. Used by permission. All rights reserved.

Scripture taken from **THE MESSAGE**, copyright © 1993, 1994, 1995, 1996, 2000, 2001, 2002. Used by permission.

THE HOLY BIBLE, NEW INTERNATIONAL VERSION®, NIV® Copyright © 1973, 1978, 1984, 2011 by Biblica, Inc.™ Used by permission. All rights reserved worldwide.

The King James Version (KJV) of the Bible is in the public domain.

www.ingramcontent.com/pod-product-compliance
Lightning Source LLC
LaVergne TN
LVHW041612070426
835507LV00008B/204